FOOTBALL SKILLS FOR YOUNG ATHLETES

Master Passing, Catching, Tackling, Running, Defense, and So Much More!

JACK RYDELL

Copyright 2025.

SPOTLIGHT MEDIA

ISBN: 978-1-951806-68-2

For questions, please reach out to:

Support@ActivityWizo.com

All Rights Reserved.

No part of this book may be reproduced or transmitted in any form or by any means, electronic or mechanical, including photocopying, recording, or by any other form without written permission from the publisher.

FREE BONUS

SCAN TO GET OUR NEXT BOOK FOR FREE!

TABLE OF CONTENTS

INTRODUCTION 1
    ELEVEN PLAYERS WORKING AS ONE 2
    BUILDING A DIVERSE TOOLBOX OF SKILLS 3
    MAKING MEMORIES FOR A LIFETIME 4
    WHAT TO EXPECT 4

CHAPTER ONE: THE BASICS OF AMERICAN FOOTBALL 7
    AN OVERVIEW OF THE RULES OF FOOTBALL 8
    SCORING IN FOOTBALL 10
    KEY POSITIONS ON THE FOOTBALL FIELD 12
    OFFENSIVE POSITIONS 13
    DEFENSIVE POSITIONS 15
    SPECIAL TEAMS POSITIONS 17
    FOOTBALL REQUIRES THREE IMPORTANT TRAITS 18
    THE IMPORTANCE OF SAFETY IN FOOTBALL 21

CHAPTER TWO: THE FUNDAMENTAL SKILLS OF FOOTBALL
.... 23
    FUNDAMENTAL OFFENSIVE SKILLS 24
    FUNDAMENTAL DEFENSIVE SKILLS 27
    GETTING STARTED WITH DRILLS 31

CHAPTER THREE: BECOMING A VERSATILE OFFENSIVE PLAYER 35

 THROWING THE FOOTBALL ACCURATELY 36

 RUNNING ACCURATE WIDE RECEIVER ROUTES 39

 SEEING THE FIELD AS A RUNNING BACK 40

 PROTECTING THE QUARTERBACK 42

 THE IMPORTANCE OF BALL SECURITY 43

 CONE DRILLS ARE FOR EVERY POSITION 45

CHAPTER FOUR: LEARNING TO PLAY LOCK-DOWN DEFENSE 49

 THE TWO BIG KEYS OF TACKLING 50

 COVERING POTENTIAL RECEIVERS PROPERLY 52

 EFFECTIVELY RUSHING THE PASSER 54

 DEFENSE IS ALL ABOUT ANGLES 56

 RECOGNIZING FORMATIONS TO READ THE OFFENSE ... 58

 THERE IS NO SUBSTITUTE FOR EFFORT 60

CHAPTER FIVE: BUILDING KEY SKILLS AT EVERY POSITION 63

 QUARTERBACKS HAVE TO MAKE QUICK DECISIONS 64

 MAKING CONTESTED CATCHES AS A WIDE RECEIVER . 66

 HOW LINEBACKERS GET RID OF BLOCKERS 68

 DEFENSIVE BACKS CHANGE GAMES WITH INTERCEPTION 69

 THE LASER FOCUS OF A KICKER 71

CHAPTER SIX: DEVELOPING FITNESS & AGILITY 75

STRENGTH TRAINING IS ESSENTIAL ON THE GRIDIRON 77

SPEED WORK CAN'T BE OVERLOOKED 78

BUILDING THE ENDURANCE TO PLAY FOUR QUARTERS 80

FLEXIBILITY IS OFTEN OVERLOOKED BY FOOTBALL PLAYERS 82

TRAINING HAPPENS IN THE OFFSEASON 83

CHAPTER SEVEN: MASTERING THE MENTAL GAME 87

KNOWING HOW TO STUDY FOOTBALL FILM 89

BUILDING CONFIDENCE ON THE FIELD 91

PLAY RECOGNITION: WILL IT BE A RUN OR A PASS? 93

THE ART OF EFFECTIVE LEADERSHIP IN FOOTBALL 95

BOUNCING BACK FROM INEVITABLE ADVERSITY 96

CHAPTER EIGHT: COMMUNICATION CREATES STRONG TEAMS 99

USING ON-FIELD SIGNALS EFFECTIVELY 101

DELIVERING INSTRUCTIONS IN THE HUDDLE 102

EVERY PLAYER NEEDS TO FILL A ROLE 104

SUPPORTING TEAMMATES ON THE FIELD 106

BONDING AWAY FROM THE GRIDIRON 107

CHAPTER NINE: DRILLS & ROUTINES TO BUILD SKILLS .. 111

SOLO DRILLS ARE GREAT FOR THE OFFSEASON 113

PARTNER DRILLS CAN BUILD IMPORTANT SKILLS 115

TEAM DRILLS ARE THE BEST PREPARATION FOR GAME ACTION 117

SPECIAL TEAMS DRILLS CAN MAKE ALL THE DIFFERENCE 119

CONDITIONING DRILLS ARE A NECESSARY EVIL 121

SCHEDULING RECOVERY INTO THE PROCESS 124

CONCLUSION 127

BECOMING A WELL-ROUNDED FOOTBALL PLAYER 129

APPROACHING THE GAME WITH HUMILITY & RESPECT 130

USING GOALS TO DRIVE GROWTH 132

EVERY FOOTBALL JOURNEY STARTS SMALL 134

INTRODUCTION

Football is the most popular game in the United States. There are over one million high school football players across the country each season, and hundreds of millions are fans of professional and college teams. Although baseball is traditionally called the "national pastime," it is football that has truly captured the heart of America.

For young athletes, there is a lot to love about this game. First, it's great for physical development. Football requires a combination of strength and speed that encourages players to work on all parts of their bodies. Every position on the field demands athleticism, flexibility, and toughness.

The mental development that occurs on a football field might be even more important than physical growth. It is the ultimate team sport. Players learn to work together with others, develop discipline, and overcome numerous adversities along the way. The game isn't easy, but that's precisely what makes it so special.

ELEVEN PLAYERS WORKING AS ONE

A single player dominates some sports. Tiger Woods, in golf, for example, became a legend thanks to his incredible skills. Even in a team sport like basketball, Michael Jordan became an iconic figure primarily due to his own efforts. His teammates played a role in winning championships, but Air Jordan is a global superstar because of what he could do with the ball in his hands.

Football is different. There are still stars like Tom Brady and Patrick Mahomes, but no one goes anywhere in this game without a team. Even the most talented quarterback would be absolutely hopeless without a great offensive line, a strong running back, and fast wide receivers. Only when the whole picture comes together are football teams able to succeed.

Young athletes can learn great lessons from the team-first nature of football. Putting teammates first and working together for a common goal is a concept that can be applied for a lifetime. Youth football players often become leaders off the field, excelling in the classroom and at home. It might be "just" a game, but it has so much to offer beyond what is shown on the scoreboard.

BUILDING A DIVERSE TOOLBOX OF SKILLS

One-dimensional football players rarely get to see the field. No matter what position is played, a collection of different skills is needed to perform well, game after game. As this book unfolds, it will become clear that building the various skills required to be a good player takes focus, consistency, and dedication.

At the professional level, nearly every player specializes in one specific position, either on offense or defense. Young players don't have to be so precise, however. It's great to learn both offensive and defensive skills, so that as many options as possible remain open. This book will support that goal by providing many different tips and drills that young players on both sides of the ball can use.

MAKING MEMORIES FOR A LIFETIME

There are sure to be plenty of ups and downs over the course of a football career. Some games will be won in thrilling fashion, while others will be heartbreaking losses. Over time, the importance of those final scores will fade, but the memories and connections made on the gridiron will never fade.

Ultimately, football is about people. Playing this game together with others is a life-changing experience that should be cherished. By working hard at the game and applying the ideas presented in the following chapters, playing football can become a lasting source of pride and a lifelong passion.

WHAT TO EXPECT

For anyone new to football, the game can be a little intimidating. There is so much to learn, and so many skills to develop. That's where this book can become a valuable resource. By breaking down the many components of football into basic, fundamental tips and drills, this book will help young players at any stage of development take the next step forward.

This is not meant to be a passive resource, however. It's not the kind of book to just read once and put back on the shelf. It's meant to guide activity and action. The advice can be implemented immediately, whether during solo training sessions or team practices. Along the way, there will even be some highlights from famous moments and players in football history, to provide a little extra boost of motivation and excitement.

Learning about football and building skills is almost as exhilarating as playing in an actual game. If this book can contribute even in a small way to improving the experience of young players across the United States, it will have been a complete success. It's time to get started!

CHAPTER ONE:
THE BASICS OF AMERICAN FOOTBALL

At first glance, this appears to be a straightforward game. Two teams oppose each other on a field that is one hundred yards long, with the goal of moving the ball all the way down the field and into the other team's end zone. The team with the most points on the board at the end of four quarters is declared the winner.

Of course, while the concept is simple, numerous rules, techniques, and strategies come into play within the game. It's important to understand the big picture of how the game works before getting into the specific skills that will be covered in the rest of this book.

AN OVERVIEW OF THE RULES OF FOOTBALL

At the core of the game of football is the concept of a "play." Unlike a sport like basketball, where play is continuous back and forth on the court, football is structured to proceed one play at a time. When the person with the ball is tackled or goes out of bounds, or when a pass is dropped, that play is over, and the teams reset for the next one. This process repeats itself over and over until the game is finished.

SOME BASIC CONCEPTS

In football, each play is called a "down." By rule, the offensive team has four downs to gain at least ten yards in the direction of the opponent's endzone. If they don't gain at least ten yards after those four downs, the ball goes to the other team, and their offense gets to take the field.

If the offense hasn't gained ten yards after three plays, it will be fourth down. At this point, they can either attempt to gain the remaining yards or choose to punt the ball away to the other team. This choice means they are giving up possession, but the punt can move the ball down the field and make it harder for the other team to score once their offense takes the field. So, it's a strategic decision to either choose to go for it on fourth down or to punt the ball away.

The game is divided into four quarters, with a halftime break taken after two quarters are completed. One team receives a kickoff to start the game, and the other team receives a kickoff to start the third quarter. There is no reset after the first and third quarters end; the game simply picks up where it left off.

It is standard in most football leagues to allow each team to take up to three timeouts per half. These timeouts can be used at any time and play a significant role in the game's strategy. A coach might use one to help his team recover after a long play, or to stop the clock close to the end of the game.

THE LAYOUT OF THE FIELD

A standard football field is one hundred yards long, not including the end zones. Those end zones are an additional ten yards long on both ends of the field, meaning the total playing surface is 120 yards long. A standard field for professional football is 160 feet wide, which also tends to be the norm at lower levels of the game.

There are lines across the field every five yards to help mark the progress of the ball as it moves up and down the field. During a game, there will be people on the sidelines who are responsible for moving the first down markers. These markers are the official measurement of where the ball needs to reach to earn a first down.

Behind each endzone is a set of goal posts. These posts have two uprights connected by a crossbar. To make a field goal (or extra point), a kick needs to fly over the crossbar and between the uprights. The dimensions of a goal post will vary based on the level of football played.

SCORING IN FOOTBALL

The winner of a football game is the team with the highest score at the end of four quarters. Professional games are played with fifteen-minute quarters, although shorter quarters are commonly used for youth games. Teams can score points in a few different ways:

TOUCHDOWNS: SIX POINTS

Touchdowns are the best way to score in football. When the offense takes the ball across the goal line and into the end zone, it counts as a touchdown, and six points are given to that team. The rules allow the offense to run the ball into the end zone by carrying it, or it can be thrown into the end zone and caught by an offensive player. Either way works. Sometimes, teams will get a touchdown by slowly working the ball down the field, one short play at a time. In other cases, it will be one big play that dramatically breaks free from the defense and makes it all the way to the endzone. Long touchdowns are some of the most exciting moments and memorable plays in all of sports.

EXTRA POINTS: ONE POINT

After scoring a touchdown, the offense is allowed to make a short kick for one extra point. The length of the kick depends on the level of football being played. Extra points are longer in the NFL than they are in high school football, for example.

TWO POINT CONVERSIONS: TWO POINTS

Instead of trying the extra point kick, the offense has the option of going for two points by running another play. This play has to get into the end zone again to score two points. Most leagues require this play to start from the two-yard line. Going for two is a common strategy late in the game when a team is behind and needs to score as many points as possible to catch up quickly.

FIELD GOALS: THREE POINTS

Not every possession will lead to a touchdown for the offense. It's hard to make progress against a tough defense, so the offense might get stopped somewhere in the field short of the end zone. When that happens, a field goal might be a possibility. A field goal is a kick that goes through the uprights, and it counts for three points. The offense needs to be close enough to the end zone to try a field goal. Even the best kickers in the NFL can only make kicks from around fifty to sixty yards. In youth football, even a field goal of thirty yards can be a challenge.

SAFETY: TWO POINTS

The last way to score points in football is to record a safety. A safety is called when the offensive player with the ball is tackled in their own end zone. A safety isn't a common play, but it is an exciting moment for the defense to be able to stop the offense so far back on the field that they end up in the other end zone. The team that scored the safety on defense then gets to receive the ball on a free kick and take over on offense.

So, there are five total ways to score points in a game of football. Obviously, a touchdown delivers the most points, but any type of scoring will go a long way toward helping to win a game. Many football games come down to the last few plays with the score very close, so every chance to score along the way is a golden opportunity.

KEY POSITIONS ON THE FOOTBALL FIELD

Eleven players for each team take the field for every play during a football game. Those players all have unique roles and are assigned specific positions. The set of positions that need to be filled is different for the offense than they are for the defense.

As a young player, it's important to learn as much about every position on the field as possible. There will be time later to specialize and pick out a position that will become a primary focus. For now, learning about what everyone does on the field and how they contribute to the team's success will create a better understanding of the game as a whole.

OFFENSIVE POSITIONS

The positions that make up the offensive side of the ball can be divided into five categories. While the goal of the offensive team is always to move the ball down the field and into the end zone, only one player can have the ball at a time. That means the rest of the players are performing other duties to help the ball carrier stay away from the defense and make as much progress as possible toward a touchdown.

QUARTERBACK

Without a doubt, this is the most vital position in football. The quarterback is the leader of the offense, and typically the leader of the team. To start each play, the quarterback receives the snap from the center and can then hand the ball to a running back, throw it to a receiver, or keep it and try to run. While it's essential to have quality players at all positions, everything starts with the quarterback. Without a good quarterback, a football team is usually doomed to a losing season.

RUNNING BACK

The running back stands behind, or next to, the quarterback at the start of each play. As the name suggests, this position is often responsible for running the ball. The quarterback can hand the ball off, and this player will run toward the end zone, trying to avoid defensive players along the way. On passing plays, the running back will turn into a blocker, trying to keep the quarterback safe while he is throwing the ball.

WIDE RECEIVERS

These players are the usual targets for the quarterback when throwing a pass. They will run out into the defensive area and try to find an open space where the quarterback can throw to them. It is important for wide receivers to be fast runners, and it is also helpful if they are tall enough to reach over the defense and make a catch. On a running play, wide receivers will also be asked to help block the defense and make room for the running back to move forward.

OFFENSIVE LINE

The offensive line is a group of five players tasked with specifically blocking the biggest players on the defense. Members of the offensive line rarely, if ever, actually carry the ball. The center is in the middle of the offensive line, with guards on either side of him, and then tackles on the ends of the line. Even the best quarterback isn't going to perform well without a strong offensive line to offer protection.

TIGHT ENDS

Finally, tight ends are players who combine the skills of offensive linemen and wide receivers. They line up on the end of the offensive line at the start of a play, but the rules permit them to run out and catch passes. It takes an incredible combination of athletic abilities to be a good tight end. This player needs to be both big and strong enough to block the defense, but also fast enough to get open and catch a pass from the quarterback.

Several different combinations of these positions can be used to reach the total of eleven players on the field for each play. There will always be a quarterback, of course, along with five offensive linemen. That accounts for six of the positions available. The remaining five will be some combination of running backs, wide receivers, and tight ends. Here are a few possible combinations:

- One running back, three wide receivers, and one tight end
- Two running backs, two wide receivers, and one tight end
- No running backs, four wide receivers, and one tight end
- One running back, two wide receivers, and two tight ends

Each team has a unique set of plays that it uses, and those plays call for various combinations of offensive players to attack the defense strategically.

DEFENSIVE POSITIONS

Four general categories of positions exist on the defensive side of football. It's not easy to stop a well-organized offense with a collection of skilled players, so a successful defense must be both strong and well-coordinated. Each player has to perform their role properly to prevent the offense from scoring and regain possession of the ball.

DEFENSIVE LINEMEN

These players line up directly across from the offensive line and are ready to go to battle on each play. Defensive linemen need to be extremely strong, and they are some of the biggest players on the field. It's also important for players on the line to be quick with their feet, so they can get around the offensive line and chase down the quarterback.

LINEBACKERS

The defense will typically use at least two linebackers on each play, but usually there will be three or four on the field. They stand behind the defensive line at the snap and have to be ready to go in any direction. A linebacker might be stopping a running back on one play before chasing down a wide receiver on the next. Linebackers are often considered the best overall athletes on the field because of the many different things they have to do.

CORNERBACKS

It is the job of a cornerback to line up in front of a wide receiver and try to prevent them from catching a pass. Cornerbacks have to be fast and physical above all else. When it's a running play, the cornerback will need to get away from the receiver and help stop the running back as he heads up the field.

SAFETIES

There are often two safeties on the field for a given play. They line up far back in the defense and are responsible for helping the cornerbacks cover the receivers. Good safeties will also come up closer to the line on some occasions to help blitz the quarterback or stop the running back. Like cornerbacks, these players need to be fast, while still having enough strength to tackle effectively.

Playing any defensive position in football is a difficult job. The offense works hard to develop plays that are tricky and hard to stop. Defensive players need to understand offensive strategy enough to predict what the other team might do and position themselves correctly to stop it.

SPECIAL TEAMS POSITIONS

There are a few specialty positions in football that don't fit into the category of offense or defense. These are known as special teams positions. The players who take the field on special teams are involved in the three types of kicking plays. Those are kickoffs, punts, and field goals (which include extra points).

Some positions on special teams overlap with those on offense and defense. For instance, the offensive and defensive lines are essentially the same. There are three unique positions, however, that only take the field when a kick is in order.

KICKER

This player has two specific jobs within special teams. First, they are responsible for the kickoffs that send the ball to the other team at the start of the game or half, and after a score. Also, this is the player who kicks the ball on a field goal or an extra point attempt.

PUNTER

As the name suggests, a punter is responsible for every punt. A punt is a different style of kicking than for kickoffs and field goals, so the two jobs are often done by two different players. However, in youth leagues, one player might be given both jobs.

RETURNER

Every football team needs a few fast players to work as returners on punts or kickoffs, which is usually not the only job a player has on a team. The returner might also play another position that requires plenty of speed, like wide receiver or cornerback.

For a young football player, excelling on special teams is a great way to earn a spot on the field. Coaches are always looking for players who are willing and able to do a great job in this area of the game. It's often overlooked, but special teams make a significant difference between winning and losing.

FOOTBALL REQUIRES THREE IMPORTANT TRAITS

This book delves into the many specific skills that young players need to develop in order to thrive on the football field. Football is a challenging and physical game, but one of the most rewarding parts of the journey is learning how to contribute positively to the team. The chapters that follow are going to get into the details of offensive and defensive skills, drills, physical fitness, mental preparation, and more.

Before getting to that point, it's important to take a moment now to highlight three high-level traits that all young football players should aim to build. These aren't specific skills, but rather broad concepts that will serve every player well throughout their football journey.

TEAMWORK

It is often said that football is the ultimate team game. No player, no matter how talented, would be hopeless on their own against the eleven players on the other side. It's only when a team comes together as a coordinated unit that it is able to score points and defeat the opponent. Each individual player is responsible for contributing to the team, rather than focusing on their own success. Selfishness has no place in this game. After all, only one player can have the ball at a time, so everyone else needs to be doing their part to chip in and help that teammate work toward the end zone. Whether in practice or a game, focusing on helping others is what football is all about.

DISCIPLINE

Improvement demands ongoing, consistent work. Football is not a game that a player can master through occasional practice and modest effort. Building skills and developing the necessary physical fitness don't come easily. Players work for all twelve months of the year, not just during football season, to improve their skills at the game. Discipline is a necessary trait to keep putting in the hard work. It's not always fun. But going through the trying times makes the fun times that much more rewarding.

RESILIENCE

Football is a difficult game. There are sure to be ups and downs along the way. For example, injuries are an inevitable part of such a physical game. Getting hurt is frustrating, and it would be easy to give up in the aftermath of an injury that keeps a player off the field for an extended time. And that is why resilience becomes such a crucial piece of the puzzle. A resilient football player comes back time after time. It could be recovering from an injury and getting back on the field. It could be dealing with a frustrating loss and moving on to get ready for the next game. Sometimes, resilience is needed when a player is benched or doesn't get as much playing time as they would like. Whatever is faced in this game, getting through it builds character and will have benefits for every other part of life.

The good news is that these three traits are all things that young football players can develop and improve. It's not necessary to be born with these characteristics. Through consistent work and practice, both off and on the field, young players can become the types of individuals that coaches love to have on their teams.

THE IMPORTANCE OF SAFETY IN FOOTBALL

It's no secret that football is a dangerous game. Injuries are a part of this sport, and that can't be ignored. For young players, it's important to understand the risks so the right steps can be taken to make playing football as safe as possible.

The first step toward safety is always to use equipment properly. While on the field, a helmet should be worn with the chinstrap secured. A mouthguard should be in at all times, as well, and all pads should be in their proper location. Getting lazy with equipment is a recipe for disaster, either in practice or in a game.

Learning proper technique is another step in the right direction. One of the key fundamentals to staying safe on the field is heads-up tackling. This technique means that the defender should always keep his head up and look at the player he is attempting to tackle. Many of the most serious football injuries occur when the defender's head drops before contact. Ideally, the head is kept up and away from the contact while the shoulders and arms do most of the work. Players should also be encouraged to report injuries to coaches immediately so they can receive the proper treatment.

Finally, warming up properly is another crucial aspect of staying safe in this game. Simply running straight out onto the field without a warm-up session can lead to injuries like pulled muscles. Even just a few minutes of gentle stretching and light jogging will go a long way toward preventing these types of issues.

Toughness is a big part of football, but that doesn't mean players should be reckless. For this sport to be enjoyed, injuries need to be avoided as much as possible. Every young player should learn safe habits from a young age so that those habits can be carried on for as long as they choose to keep playing the game.

CHAPTER TWO:
THE FUNDAMENTAL SKILLS OF FOOTBALL

The skills used on a football field are particular to individual positions. A quarterback needs an entirely different set of skills from a defensive lineman, for example. With that said, young players should develop as many different skills as possible from various positions throughout the field.

Learning how to do everything early on will open up options as the player gets older. Specialization is inevitable as a football journey goes along, but at the start, trying everything out and learning the fundamentals is a great strategy (and a lot of fun).

This chapter will introduce some of the fundamental skills used on both sides of the ball. Players who are new to the game can practice these skills and start building their confidence at multiple positions. This experience highlights the fun of being a football player!

FUNDAMENTAL OFFENSIVE SKILLS

Two categories of skills are critical on the offensive side of the ball. One category is skills that relate to actually handling and throwing the ball. The other category relates to blocking for the person who is carrying the ball. Since everyone blocks at one time or another, and anyone can end up with the ball, all players should be trained in these two disciplines.

HOW TO HANDLE THE FOOTBALL

If there is one thing that's certain in this game, it's that someone on defense is always trying to take the ball away. Defenders are trained to attack the ball and try to wrestle it away from the offense (more on that skill later). So, of course, offensive players need to learn how to keep a tight grip on the ball whenever they are carrying it.

Football coaches drill offensive players on always holding the ball "high and tight." This phrase means the ball should be held high up on the chest with the elbow of the arm bent at roughly ninety degrees. When the ball is tight to the chest and high up on the body, it's much harder for a defender to pry it away.

It's good practice to simply walk around holding the ball in this position as much as possible. A player doesn't even need to be at football practice to work on this skill. The more time the player spends holding onto the ball in this powerful position, the more comfortable and natural it will become. A good "high and tight" position doesn't eliminate the possibility of a fumble, but it does make things harder on the defense.

The other key to handling the football is holding the ball with both hands when going into a congested area of the field. When a running back attempts to run through the line, for example, they will often use both hands on the ball to give it a bear hug. That move makes it nearly impossible for the defense to get the ball. It's harder to run fast when holding the ball with two hands, but that's a trade that's worth making. Few things in football are as crucial as ball security. Holding tightly with two hands while being tackled will help the player avoid fumbles and keep the offense moving right along.

BLOCKING THE DEFENSE

No matter which player on the offense has the ball, the defensive players are immediately going to be sprinting toward that player to get them on the ground. Without good blocking, even the most elusive runner will have a hard time shaking the entire defense alone. It's when the rest of the offense does a great job blocking that the ball carrier can make a break for the end zone.

All players on the football field should know how to block properly. Learning this skill at a young age will make a player far more valuable. Every coach loves having players who understand the fundamentals of blocking techniques. One common misconception among young football players is that only certain positions, such as linemen, need to focus on developing their blocking skills. However, everyone on the field will be asked to block at one point or another, so this is a fundamental skill that should always be prioritized.

Good blocking starts with proper positioning. The player's feet need to be in the right position to get in front of the defender and effectively slow him down. Yes, blocking is done with the hands, but it really starts with the lower body. When the offensive player has a good base and is in the proper position, putting hands on the defense and making a solid block becomes pretty simple.

Taking small, quick steps is the best way to get in front of the defense. Shuffling the feet from side to side with choppy steps allows for precise positioning adjustments while aiming for the defender's chest. Then, as contact is made, the player should have his hands up at chest height. Putting two hands on the chest of the defender, without holding, can stop that defender from moving forward and getting to the ball carrier.

The concept of aggressive blocking is crucial for all offensive players to consider. Defenders are trying to avoid blocks, of course, and they'll fight back with their own hands when getting engaged with the offense. So, good blockers take the fight to the defense, aggressively seeking out contact. It actually doesn't take a long block to do a great job. Even slowing up a defender for just a moment could be enough for a running back or wide receiver to get around the defender and head down the field for a first down.

FUNDAMENTAL DEFENSIVE SKILLS

Just as with the offensive side of the ball, there are two core fundamental defensive skills that young players should develop. Several other skills are also required, which will be covered later in the book. Starting with these two key abilities will create a foundation for a young defensive player to build on moving forward.

TACKLING THE BALL CARRIER

Tackling the ball carrier is the goal of the defense on every play. Whichever player on the offense has the ball, everyone on the defense will be trying to tackle him as soon as possible. Quick and consistent tackling is the foundation of the defense and what enables a team to prevent first downs and regain possession for their own offense to score.

The first piece of the tackling puzzle is getting into position to reach the ball carrier and pulling him down to the ground. It's impossible to tackle a player who is out of reach, after all. Good defensive players are not only fast, but they also understand the right angles to take to catch up to the ball carrier.

Running directly at the player with the ball will typically leave a defender a step or two behind and out of the play. Instead, it's important to anticipate where the offensive player is going to be after a few more steps, so the defender can cut him off and hopefully make a tackle. Of course, this strategy works best when multiple defenders work in unison to chase down the player with the ball. It's pretty easy for a good runner to avoid a single defender in open space, but it's much harder to keep moving down the field when multiple defenders are in position to make the tackle together.

Once in position, there is a simple mantra that highlights the key factor of how tackling works: low man wins. This phrase means that the player who gets lower between the ball carrier and the defender is usually the one who will win the encounter. If the defender establishes a low center of gravity while hitting the ball carrier, he will typically be able to knock him down and complete the tackle. However, if the defender comes in high, the hit is likely to be a glancing blow, and the ball carrier may keep running.

Few things in football drive coaches crazy quite like high tackling. It is seen as a lazy habit and a poor technique. One of the best ways for a young player to stand out to coaches on the defensive side of the ball is to always bend their knees and get low when tackling. Using this technique will limit the number of missed tackles and make the player a reliable member of the defensive unit.

READING THE OFFENSE

The mental challenges of playing defense in football might be even bigger than the physical challenges. Every offense spends tons of time and effort trying to build plays that are confusing and complicated. It's the job of the defense to sort through all the distractions and figure out where the ball is going to go once it is snapped.

Great defensive players, surprisingly, end up becoming experts on offensive football. They understand what the other team is likely to do given the situation at hand. If it's third down and only one yard to go, certain plays are more likely than others. Specifically, a running play will often be called. On the other hand, if it's third and long, the offense is very likely to pass the ball.

It's never too early in a football journey to start learning as much as possible about offensive strategy. Players who want to excel on defense should watch film from past games and learn about the tendencies of certain players and coaches. There is usually one player on the field for the offense who is the fastest and hardest to tackle. That player will get the ball frequently, but they may also be used as a decoy on some plays. Defenses have to figure all of this out quickly to run in the right direction to tackle the ball carrier before too much yardage is gained.

Different positions on the defense will have different jobs in terms of reading the offensive attack. Linebackers are at the heart of the action, and they need to understand formations and recognize the differences between pass and run setups. The defensive linemen are more concerned with how the offensive line will block. Will they use a double team on a certain rusher? Are they going to pull a guard for a running play? From a distance, line play looks like a wrestling match, but there is actually a lot of strategy going on in there.

For cornerbacks and safeties, the first concern is preventing big pass plays. These positions require an understanding of wide receiver route patterns. The coach will decide whether to use a zone or man-to-man defense. While primarily concerned with the wide receivers, these perimeter players also need to keep an eye on the backfield so they can come up and tackle a running back quickly after a handoff.

The great thing about learning offensive strategy is that this work can be done at any time. A player doesn't need to be on the field to add to their knowledge. Watching replays of old games or films from a recent practice can be an educational opportunity and a chance to improve. The best defensive players tend to be those who not only have physical tools but also an understanding of how the game works.

GETTING STARTED WITH DRILLS

Perhaps no sport uses as many drills as football. Whether during formal practice or on off days, football players are constantly going through drills to improve a specific skill. Knowing as many different types of drills as possible and practicing them regularly can help a player improve significantly from one season to the next.

This book presents numerous drills throughout its various sections. For now, the list below presents some basic drills that can help players across the field get better. Once a player starts to settle into a specific position, more specialized drills can be performed to refine the skills required at that spot on the field.

TENNIS BALL CATCHES

Hand-eye coordination is important in virtually every sport. Football is no different. Players need to be as adept as possible at using their hands, whether it's to snatch the ball out of the air or bring another player to the ground. One way to work on this away from the field is by using tennis balls to create a quick catching drill. Two players can toss tennis balls quickly back and forth, altering the ball's location to make the catches more challenging. This drill won't necessarily feel like football practice, but that's exactly what it is. Five minutes of catching tennis balls will be a step toward better coordination and an improved ability to make a key grab when it is needed most.

STANCE REHEARSAL

Another easy drill to perform away from the football field is simply working on both the two-point and three-point football stance that starts each play. These stances are used by a variety of players and must be mastered by every young player. A two-point stance is one where only the feet are on the ground. It is often employed by players at the end of the offensive line, but not always. The three-point stance involves placing one hand on the ground to lower the player's position. It's possible to practice taking these stances anywhere, and even doing a few repetitions of getting into and out of the stance will be a big help once practice and game time roll around.

LADDER DRILLS

This drill does require a bit of equipment, but ladders are easy to find and generally affordable. With an exercise ladder that can be laid on the ground, it's possible to do various footwork drills whenever a few minutes are available. Since footwork is such a big part of football, at every position, it's great to spend time regularly doing ladder work. Any type of drill that requires the player to move quickly through the ladder while moving their feet in a coordinated pattern is a good one. Doing high knees through the ladder is a classic drill, as are side shuffles. For defensive players, backpedaling through the ladder is also helpful.

The lesson that there is no offseason in football should be learned at a young age by every player. Recognizing that there is always room for improvement, regardless of the season, can motivate young players to strive for new heights. Performing drills, even if they are done alone, is the foundational work that can ultimately lead to amazing results when the lights are brightest.

CHAPTER THREE: BECOMING A VERSATILE OFFENSIVE PLAYER

A theme that will run through this book is versatility. It's critical for a young player on the gridiron. There is simply no need to specialize at a young age in this sport. It's too early for a young player to know exactly what their physical skills will look like later on, so the only smart strategy is to learn as much about as many different positions as possible.

That's what this chapter is all about. Each section that follows will break down one of the specific skills required to play a given position on offense. There will be even more detail provided in a later chapter on how players at various positions can reach their full potential, but this is a good starting point. A young football player who works on developing these various talents will give themselves plenty of opportunities moving forward in one way or another.

THROWING THE FOOTBALL ACCURATELY

An accurate pass is almost impossible to cover. Sure, throwing the football hard is helpful for a quarterback, as well, but there is nothing quite like a throw that drops to the receiver at exactly the right spot. Even good defense is pretty much hopeless against this kind of pass. It's no coincidence that some of the greatest football players of all time, names like Tom Brady and Peyton Manning, were also some of the most accurate throwers of all time.

Accurate throwing doesn't happen by coincidence or accident. It takes consistent, regular practice. Fortunately, that practice is pretty simple. It comes down to getting as many repetitions as possible, throwing the ball toward targets on the field. Those targets could be actual receivers, or even just garbage cans placed in spots where balls are commonly thrown to during games.

A significant element of timing is involved with throwing accurate passes. The quarterback and receiver have to be on the same page and understand the timing of the route for the ball to end up at the right spot at the right time. However, before any of that matters, the quarterback needs to be able to deliver the ball where he wants to put it. Once that skill is established, then the timing with the receivers can come into play.

While working through numerous throwing repetitions, the following fundamentals can be monitored to make sure the quarterback is giving himself the best possible chance to put the ball right on target.

THROWING FROM THE GROUND UP

Some young football players are surprised to learn just how important the legs are to making great throws. Accurate throws start with solid, repeatable footwork. The feet should be taking short, choppy steps to make minor adjustments before the ball is launched in the direction of a receiver. Professional quarterbacks will often work just on footwork, without a ball in sight. Mastering how the feet move will not only make a quarterback more accurate but will also help him avoid rushing defenders.

A SHORT ARM ACTION

It's tempting to bring over throwing skills from a game like baseball and implement them into football. After all, baseball is all about throwing accurately, so it would seem like that skill would translate perfectly to football. Shouldn't a young athlete who also plays baseball just bring that throwing technique over to play quarterback? Not exactly. The throwing action used in baseball is usually longer, with the arm reaching way back and turning the ball away from the target before it is whipped forward. That's not the ideal way to throw a football. Good quarterbacks keep the arm swing short, and the front point of the football is always pointing generally toward the target. A long arm action in football leads to a slow release and inaccurate passes. When the arm motion is nice and short, it quickly becomes much easier to put the ball precisely where it needs to be.

EYES DOWN THE FIELD

Accurate passing is directly related to eye control. Specifically, this means looking at the spot where the ball needs to be delivered. If the quarterback is looking elsewhere, such as down at the ground or right at a defender, it will be hard to place the ball correctly. This technique should be practiced during accuracy drills. The eyes of a young quarterback should always be up, scanning the field to see where the ball is going to go. It's going to be even harder during a game to maintain eye discipline in the face of a rushing defender, so it's critical to nail this fundamental detail in practice.

A quarterback who can accurately throw the ball is going to grab the attention of a coach quickly. That's a relatively rare skill, and one that highlights players who are serious about becoming good quarterbacks.

RUNNING ACCURATE WIDE RECEIVER ROUTES

The first inclination of a young wide receiver is to simply run fast. By sprinting down the field, it seems like getting open is inevitable. That's not how it works. The defense is fast, too, and without accurate route running, a receiver will rarely find himself open enough to become the quarterback's chosen target.

There is another problem with simply running fast: the quarterback won't know where the receiver is going to end up. Those two need to be on the same page to complete a pass. When the wide receiver can run the route as described in the playbook, the quarterback will be able to release the ball with confidence.

A couple of essential components come together to create a solid route. The first is a clean release. Wide receivers should get off the line quickly as soon as the ball is snapped. Exploding off the line will immediately put the defender on his heels. Defenses often try to "jam" or block the receiver right off the line, so getting a powerful, clean release into a route is an important skill to have.

Once the release is completed, it's about knowing the route and timing the moves perfectly. The quarterback is counting on a certain timing from the receiver, and it needs to be as consistent as possible from one repetition to the next. Good receivers need to be fast runners, of course, but they also need to be predictable runners.

The last piece of the puzzle for running routes is to come back to the ball after it is thrown. Unless the pass is a deep ball lobbed over the head of the receiver, most routes will call for the receiver to come back aggressively to snatch the ball before the defense gets it. If the receiver drifts down the field or just gets lazy and stands flat-footed, the defense will probably be able to catch up and knock down the ball. All receivers should be in the habit of coming back as the ball is in the air to shorten the distance that it has to fly before being caught.

SEEING THE FIELD AS A RUNNING BACK

What's the most crucial skill a running back needs to possess? It would certainly be tempting to say pure speed. Strength is also an important factor. It's also necessary to maintain control over the ball with a firm grip to avoid costly fumbles. There is no doubt that all of those skills are necessary, but they might fall in line behind the ability to see the field clearly as the play develops.

Seeing the field and knowing where to run to avoid defenders is what playing running back is all about. Some of the best running backs in football history weren't necessarily the fastest, but they were skilled at picking the right spot at the right time to gain some yards. When a player combines vision with other traits like speed and strength, it's a recipe for incredible results.

Learning to see the field as a running back is partially a product of experience. The more reps a young player gets at running back, the better he will become at reading the defense and picking the right hole in the line. But there are other ways to improve in this area. For one thing, young players should watch a lot of football and see what the defense tends to do when running plays. Where do the linebackers go when they know that it's a run? Do the safeties or corners come in to help tackle, and how can they be avoided? Acquiring knowledge is always an indispensable part of getting better at this game.

Of course, as vital as it is to read the defense well, there will come a point when a running back simply needs to avoid a tackler to keep moving forward. That's why lateral agility is a trait that young players should develop. The ability to stop quickly in one direction, only to accelerate in another direction, is what makes a running back stand out.

Consistently gaining yards is basically a two-part process. First, the running back needs to take the ball and pick the right hole based on what they are seeing ahead. If the correct path is selected, there will still likely be one tackler waiting to make a play. It's pretty much impossible to find a route where there is no defense in the way at all. The job of the running back is to now use athletic ability to beat that lone defender and pick up a bunch of yards.

A theme is starting to emerge as the book moves along. Football is a game that always blends physical skills with intelligence. For being such a rough and violent game, endless thinking takes place on the field. Smart decisions and proper preparation come together with raw athletic talent to achieve great things.

PROTECTING THE QUARTERBACK

Playing offensive line is often a thankless job. Many football fans take the line for granted and focus only on the players at the "skill" positions, like quarterback, running back, and receiver. It may be for this reason that many young players gravitate toward those other positions. However, playing offensive line can be a rewarding experience, and performance on the line will go a long way toward helping a team win.

Size is undoubtedly a big part of playing on the offensive line well, which really isn't the spot for small players. With that said, offensive linemen of modest size can get good results with the proper technique. And, like so many other things on the field, it all starts with the feet. Keeping your feet moving and staying balanced is critical to avoid getting knocked down and run over.

As soon as the ball is snapped, the players on the offensive line need to be moving their feet. If it is a running play, those feet will be moving forward. They'll be aggressively seeking out contact at the line, trying to engage the defensive players so the running back can go around and gain some yards. Driving powerfully into the defensive line with active feet can shift the whole play further down the field.

The approach is just the opposite when it's a pass play. In this case, the offensive line will start by dropping back slightly. This move gives the line a moment to prepare for impact as the defenders start to rush. In a balanced and athletic position, an offensive lineman can engage with a defender and try to hold off the rush as long as possible. Even if he has to give a little bit of ground as the defender pushes, the offensive lineman can still keep the quarterback safe. No rush can be held back forever. But even putting up a good fight for a few seconds can be enough to give the quarterback time to pick out an open receiver down the field.

Speaking of buying time, it's always necessary for linemen to keep leverage in mind. Good line play involves protecting the middle of the field and making the defense go around the end. It's a much longer path to the quarterback to force the rush to go around the outside, after all. When done correctly, the five-man offensive line can form a "pocket" for the quarterback to use for his passing space. By the time any of the defenders get around the outside to attack the quarterback, the ball should be long gone.

THE IMPORTANCE OF BALL SECURITY

Every coach in football says the same thing before the start of a game. "We have to protect the ball." Turnovers are killers in any game of football. It's often the case that the team with the most turnovers will lose the game, and that's no coincidence. By protecting the ball, teams maintain their chance to score while on offense, and don't give the other team extra chances to do the same thing.

For young players, understanding the importance of ball security is a great starting point. Avoiding fumbles is a top priority and should be treated that way. In other words, it's never worth it to put the ball at risk in an effort to gain a few extra yards (unless it's the last play of the game, or a situation like that). Generally speaking, ball security is number one, and everything else comes next.

Sometimes, ball security will fade as the game wears on, and players get tired. However, mental discipline should also come into play. It's essential to stay focused throughout the entire game, especially on fundamentals like controlling the ball. A single sloppy turnover due to fatigue late in the game could mean the difference between winning and losing.

Earlier in the book, the concept of "high and tight" was introduced. This method is key to avoiding fumbles. Holding the ball tightly and high on the chest makes it hard for the defense to get it. As soon as the ball starts to drop or the grip starts to loosen, an aggressive defender will come in and strip it away. Practicing this position is an important part of preparation for all players who carry the ball.

There is also something to be said for learning how to get tackled. Most plays end in a tackle, and the ball shouldn't be put at risk while going to the ground. The natural tendency when falling or being tackled is to reach out for the ground, but that would create a considerable risk of a fumble. So, young football players have to get used to going down without using their hands to brace their fall. The best way to get tackled is with two hands firmly on the ball the whole way down and onto the ground. It is unlikely that a fumble will occur at the last moment before the play is over.

CONE DRILLS ARE FOR EVERY POSITION

One thing that ties these various football positions together is the use of cone drills to sharpen skills and get ready for game day. The specifics of each drill will vary depending on the trait being developed and the position being played. However, there is no doubt that having some cones on hand is always helpful for a young football player who is driven to improve their skills.

The following list details some excellent drill options that can be incorporated into offseason training or a team practice routine.

THE "W" DRILL

This drill is a classic for wide receivers and cornerbacks. Those positions need to change direction regularly and then accelerate quickly. For corners, it's important to be able to back pedal effectively. Setting up cones in a "W" shape and then having the players move as quickly as possible through that pattern is something coaches have been doing for generations. It can also be switched up to a "Y" pattern for a slight variation. Whatever shape is used, the important thing is that the players use this drill with a sense of urgency and try to use it to increase foot speed and coordination when going through a route.

RUNNING BACKS: CUTTING & WEAVING

There is never much room for a running back to operate. Small, quick steps that avoid the linemen's legs are critical. Setting up a series of cones in a straight line that a running back can cut and swerve through is a useful drill. For example, the running back might charge straight ahead at a line of cones and alternate stepping to the right and left of every other one. The drill could also be modified with taller cones for the running back to pick his feet up and get them over and back down again. Anything that enables the player to move quickly in multiple directions can be effective.

QQUARTERBACK DROP BACK DRILLS

A consistent drop back before stepping up into the pocket is crucial for proper quarterback play. Again, here, it's cones that can come to the rescue. One cone can be placed at the spot where the drop back should end, and another can be placed in the middle of where the pocket should be. Then, over and over, the quarterback can move back to the top of the drop and then step up into the (imaginary) pocket. With enough practice, this footwork will become second nature, and the quarterback will always be in the right spot to make a great throw.

LINEMAN SHUTTLE DRILLS

Being a lineman is challenging because size and strength are needed, but it's also important to be quick. To improve quickness, a simple shuttle drill between two sets of cones might be used. Setting the cones ten to twenty feet apart, linemen can run back and forth between the two ends, touching a hand down on each turn. Adding this drill to a regular workout routine will help make a lineman more athletic than ever before. By building both strength and endurance, along with some extra quickness, a young player can quickly become a critical part of an offensive line operation.

Playing any offensive position in football can be exciting and rewarding. As the years pass and players gain more experience, it usually becomes clear which position on the gridiron is going to be their best option. They can contribute to the team's success in one area more than any other. For now, however, trying to pick up a wide variety of skills is not only useful, but it's fun. From throwing great passes to holding up on the offensive line and beyond, the abilities highlighted in this chapter will never go out of style.

CHAPTER FOUR: LEARNING TO PLAY LOCK-DOWN DEFENSE

It's common for young football players to be drawn to the offensive side of the ball. There's a lot of glory associated with scoring a touchdown, after all. However, many players find that after a little practice, they fall in love with defense. There is just something about banding together with teammates to keep the other team off the board that is a never-ending thrill.

This chapter will discuss some of the key principles for playing solid defense. Stopping the offense is far from simple, but it gets easier when the list of abilities below comes together in a single package.

THE TWO BIG KEYS OF TACKLING

At the heart of it all, defense is about tackling. Bringing down the ball carrier as soon as possible is the name of the game. When a defense tackles well, it's hard for the offense to consistently pick up first downs and keep the drive moving toward the end zone.

The two significant components of tackling properly are wrapping up and driving through the ball carrier. Having one of these two in place could lead to a successful tackle, but not always. With both in place, the player with the ball will have almost no chance to escape.

First, it's essential to understand the concept of wrapping up the ball carrier. In this context, "wrapping up" means hugging the other player using both arms and bringing him to the ground.

Football players are fast and strong, and just hitting the ball carrier won't necessarily do the job of knocking him down and completing the tackle. It's common to see missed tackles where players don't use their arms and instead just put a shoulder into the offensive player. That's a mistake that will drive coaches crazy and will lead to countless extra yards for the ball carrier over the course of a game.

Quality tackling always includes wrapping up and holding on tight. When this is done correctly, the offensive player will have to drag the entire weight of the tackling defender while still trying to move forward. That's hard to do, and even if the ball carrier does stay up for a moment, another defender should be coming along to finish things off.

Once the tackler has wrapped up the ball carrier, the other piece of the puzzle is to keep driving the feet through the tackle, which is why using sleds is such a popular technique in football practice. The sleds are heavy, forcing players to keep moving their feet to drive them forward. That's useful when trying to go through a block, and it's also crucial for making tackles. If the tackler stops as soon as he reaches the ball carrier, the wrap-up might not be enough alone to get the player down to the ground.

Stopping the feet as soon as contact is made is considered a lazy technique in the football world. The play is never over until the whistle blows, after all. Keeping the feet moving and driving hard through the ball carrier, while wrapping up, is what will allow for solid, consistent tackling to be executed both in practice and in games.

Wrapping up and driving through the tackle is a powerful combination. Any young football player who can master these two skills will be well on their way toward solid performance on the defensive side of the ball. There is, however, one additional point to add to this discussion. When tackling, it's best to hit the ball carrier low, if at all possible. Young players commonly make the mistake of going high on the ball carrier, only to get knocked off and miss the tackle. The lower body is where effective tackles can be made. This approach takes the legs out from under the ball carrier, causing them to go to the ground quickly.

COVERING POTENTIAL RECEIVERS PROPERLY

While tackling is extremely important, it's also critical to cover potential receivers when they go out on a route. If even one receiver is left open, the quarterback will find him, and a big play will be the result. And more than just the cornerbacks need to know how to cover receivers. Pretty much everyone on the defense, other than the linemen, needs to learn the fundamentals of coverage technique.

The first thing for a young football player to learn about coverage is that it's all about the hips. The hips are located in the middle of the body and indicate where the opponent is likely to run. A good offensive player will know how to use head fakes and other tricks to throw the defender off track, but the hips always tell the truth. As a coverage defender, having the discipline to focus on the hips while ignoring the other parts of the body is a significant step toward staying in position with a receiver.

While focusing on the hips, use small, choppy steps to stay close to the offensive player. Since a quick receiver or running back can change directions suddenly, keep steps small and be ready to adjust on the fly. Long strides are great for sprinting in a straight line, but that's not how coverage works. Defenders have to adjust and find a way to follow the route being run, and short steps are a great way to make that happen.

Young defenders should prioritize ladder drills during practice and offseason training. Ladder drills are popular in football precisely because of the importance of short steps. Keeping the feet moving, with short strides, makes it possible to stick to a receiver and not let them open up any space. As soon as a defender allows his feet to stop moving, the receiver will be gone, and the play will be blown open.

Like with tackling, it's also important to stay low when covering a receiver. A defender will be more balanced and agile when staying low to the ground, rather than up high. The knees should remain flexed, and the player should be in an athletic position, ready to move quickly in any direction as needed. The profile of a great coverage defender is one who is lower than the receiver, has his hands up, and his feet moving. Dialing in these fundamentals makes it possible to play great defense on the perimeter of the field.

EFFECTIVELY RUSHING THE PASSER

Nothing can disrupt an offense quite like getting pressure on the quarterback. When the defense can rush the quarterback consistently throughout a game, everything that the offense wants to do is thrown into disarray. The receivers don't have enough time to get deep into their routes. The running backs and tight ends have to stay in to help block, meaning they can't get out into routes and give the quarterback more options.

It's no wonder that coaches put such an emphasis on this part of the defense. Pressuring the quarterback is a game-changing skill. On the other hand, not pressuring the quarterback makes life very easy on the offense. The quarterback will be able to stand in the pocket and scan the field for an open receiver without worrying about being sacked. It's actually not that hard to throw the ball to a receiver for a completion when there isn't any pressure being applied. It's not an overstatement to say that pressuring the quarterback is often what determines who wins or loses in a football game.

So, how do players consistently get to the quarterback? It all starts in the weight room. Technique matters, and that will be discussed shortly, but there is no substitute for strength. A strong lineman or linebacker will be much more likely to move a blocker out of their way and get into the backfield. Also, endurance plays a role. A fit defensive player who can keep coming, play after play, all game long, is hard to deal with. If a rusher is in great shape and able to go after the quarterback in the fourth quarter when the offensive linemen are getting tired, they'll have the chance to make big plays.

Strength isn't the only physical characteristic that is needed when rushing the passer. Quickness matters as well. Specifically, the rusher needs to "get off the ball" quickly when it is snapped. Reacting quickly to the snap and getting into the rush right away can put the offensive line on its heels. Practicing this quick get-off is a key part of football training for anyone who will be rushing the passer.

A rusher also needs to develop a few moves that can be used to get around or through the line. The swim move is a popular technique that can be used in this pursuit. The idea is simple enough, and the name pretty much says it all. When the ball is snapped, the rusher pushes hard into the blocker in front of them. Then, instead of engaging fully with the blocker, the rusher will use one arm to "swim" over and around the offensive lineman. When used right, this move can make the rusher's streamlined side profile harder for the blocker to keep in front. For edge rushers, a spin move technique can also be used, where they do a 360-degree spin to get the blocker out of position and hopefully get by.

One last point about rushing the passer needs to be made, and it might be a little surprising. One key trait for all rushers is to know when to stop rushing. At some point in the play, it's going to become unlikely that the rusher will reach the quarterback, so the priorities need to change quickly. For example, if the quarterback is about to throw the ball, the rusher can stop pushing forward and instead jump up to knock down the pass. It's much harder for a quarterback to complete a pass when there is a big player in front of them jumping up with their arms extended.

Stopping a rush can also be about preventing the quarterback from escaping with his feet. Some quarterbacks are excellent runners, and if the defensive players rush too far up the field, the quarterback will simply sneak away and run down the field. So, knowing the quarterback is a running threat, it's important not to get so caught up in the rush that a running lane opens up. Of course, if scouting before the game revealed that the quarterback was a slow runner, this wouldn't be so much of an issue, and the defense could be more aggressive with the rush.

DEFENSE IS ALL ABOUT ANGLES

The players given the responsibility of carrying the ball for an offense are fast. Very fast. Whether it's a running back breaking through the line or a receiver catching a pass down the sideline, the guy with the ball can sprint down the field in the blink of an eye.

The speed typically seen on the offensive side of the ball means that defenders must understand angles properly to get the job done. In football, "angles" refers to the direction that a defender is running in an effort to catch up to the ball carrier and make a tackle. If the defender runs directly toward where the ball carrier is now, they'll always be a couple of steps behind and probably won't ever catch up. Instead, it's essential to run to where the ball carrier is likely to be in a second or two. Learning how to time these angles and get them just right is a huge part of becoming a reliable tackler.

Thinking back to the advice that was provided earlier in this chapter about tackling, none of it will matter if the offensive player is long gone when the defender arrives. It's impossible to wrap up the ball carrier without first catching him, after all. The best way to learn how to take good angles on defense is simply to play more defense. With experience, it will become easier to visualize where the ball carrier will be in the future.

It's often necessary to take an angle that will give up a few yards to avoid giving up a bigger play. For example, if a quarterback throws a pass to an open receiver down the sideline, it would be tempting for the defender to run right at the receiver and hope to make a big hit. But what if the defender doesn't arrive in time? Now the receiver will be running down the sideline and may make it all the way to the end zone.

The better approach for that defender would be to run at an angle slightly further down the field. This method will take away the possibility of a big play and will cut off the receiver before he can really get going. This play will likely result in a gain of yardage for the offense, but at least it won't be a huge play that turns into a score. Defensive teams that take poor angles are always a step behind and typically struggle to keep the opposing side off the scoreboard.

RECOGNIZING FORMATIONS TO READ THE OFFENSE

Football is played like a game of chess. Sure, it's more violent than chess, but there is just as much thinking and strategy involved. Each team is trying to stay one step ahead of the other, using schemes and tactics to trick the opponent and make some open space on the field.

For defensive players, a detailed understanding of how offensive football works is critical. Knowing what the offense is likely to try to do in various situations will help the player anticipate the play and get ahead of the action. No one can perfectly predict the plays used by another team, but having as much insight and knowledge as possible will lead to better results.

The first step for a young player is understanding down and distance. Play calling on the offensive side is largely dictated by what down it is and how far the offense needs to go to pick up the first down. For example, third and short is commonly a running down, whereas third and long will almost always be a pass. Many teams also like to establish the run and get ahead of the sticks with a first-down run, but that's far from a sure thing. As football has evolved, more and more teams pass the ball with regularity.

Along with down and distance, it's also necessary to consider the score and time of the game. Early in the game, the plays will likely be a mix of runs and passes, leaning on whatever a given team tends to do well. On the other hand, if the game is late and the team with the ball is behind, they will likely throw on nearly every down. There just isn't enough time left to run the ball and get all the way down the field. Young football players should learn as much as possible about this kind of strategic thinking so they can know what to expect before the ball is snapped.

The formation that the offense uses when they come to the line will also offer some insight into what they plan to do with the play. Some formations give away that the offense is likely to run the ball, while other formations signal a pass. A classic running formation, for example, is a line that comes in tight and features two tight ends. That means there are seven players on the line, so the offense is likely to run it. Of course, most teams will have a couple of surprising plays that lead to a pass out of this formation, but it's going to be a run most of the time.

Not surprisingly, a passing formation is usually one that is spread out with plenty of receivers. In modern football, it's not uncommon to see a formation that has four wide receivers, one running back, and no tight ends. While it's certainly possible to run out of this formation from time to time, most of the plays run out of this kind of set are going to be passes. As a defender, it's essential to watch for the adjustments the offense is making to their formation and prepare for the type of play that is likely to follow.

THERE IS NO SUBSTITUTE FOR EFFORT

Even given everything that has been discussed so far in this chapter, by far the most important thing a young player can bring to the defensive side of the ball is effort. Working hard on defense is essential, as all eleven players need to contribute to the cause if the offense is going to be stopped effectively.

Hustle is a constant focus on defense. Players can never really be sure where a play is going to go or when it will end, so hustling to the ball and tackling hard is required. Defensive players who assume the play is over and stop hustling will soon find themselves on the bench. When watching a football game, it's easy to spot a quality defensive team simply by seeing how many people are around the ball when the play ends. Did most of the defense hustle to the ball carrier to help out? That's the mark of a defense that is working hard and is going to have success.

This kind of hustle can pay off in many ways. For instance, a ball carrier might break free from what looked like a sure tackle. If the rest of the defense isn't hustling, that broken tackle could lead to a first down or even a touchdown. On the other hand, a hustling defense will have plenty of other guys nearby to bring down the ball carrier, even if the first guy misses. Even if this only happens once or twice in a game, those couple of instances could easily make the difference between winning and losing.

It's also possible that the defense can win a turnover by hustling to the ball. As one player tackles the ball carrier, the others in the area can be swiping at the ball, trying to knock it away. Turnovers change football games, unlike anything else, so it's always worth fighting for the ball and trying to get it loose. And, of course, if some of the defensive players can force a fumble, others who have hustled into the area will be in position to recover that football and give the ball back to the offense.

The power of a single player hustling throughout a game on defense goes beyond just the practical benefits discussed above. There is also the matter of inspiring everyone else on the defense to do the same. No one wants to be left behind, and when one defensive player takes the lead by hustling and playing hard all the way to the whistle, others are sure to do the same. Soon enough, that effort will spread throughout the entire team, and the unit will perform better than it would have otherwise.

For a young player, always working hard on the field is like a superpower. It's something that every coach loves, and it never goes out of style. Whatever position is being played, on either side of the ball, a full effort in every quarter will always be respected in this game.

CHAPTER FIVE: BUILDING KEY SKILLS AT EVERY POSITION

Over time, a young football player will inevitably be moved more and more in the direction of one or two specific positions. That's just how the game works. It's great for players new to the game to learn and experience as many positions as possible, but strengths and weaknesses will eventually become apparent.

For example, the size of a player will impact where they fit on the field. A large player will be a natural fit for the offensive or defensive line, while a smaller, faster player will likely land at a spot like receiver or cornerback. Size is only one of the pieces of the puzzle, however. Some players simply have a better aptitude for certain positions, as they seem to see the field best from those spots.

This chapter will delve further into the specific skills required for various positions on the field. Continuing to develop skills and settling into a position that can be mastered will foster progress and a spot on increasingly competitive teams.

QUARTERBACKS HAVE TO MAKE QUICK DECISIONS

The hardest part of playing quarterback isn't throwing the ball accurately or throwing it far, or even getting hit by a powerful linebacker who sneaks through the line. Without a doubt, the most challenging part of playing quarterback successfully is making crucial decisions in the blink of an eye. The game moves fast, and the quarterback is in charge of making the choices that will dictate how everything goes on the field. Good quarterbacks need all of the right physical traits and skills, but more than anything else, they need to make the right decisions both before and after the ball is snapped.

How fast does the quarterback need to be to get rid of the ball? It is often the case that less than three seconds pass between the snap of the ball and the release. That might sound like a lot, but it goes by in a blink. The quarterback has to take in a tremendous amount of information in a short amount of time, including where the defenders are moving, what's happening with the rush, and which receiver might be coming open. Typically, the ball needs to be thrown even before the receiver is actually open. The quarterback needs to see how things are developing and throw the ball in anticipation of a receiver getting open by the time the ball arrives.

For a fast quarterback, there is another decision that comes into the mix. In addition to deciding where to throw the ball, they must also decide whether to run or pass. Many plays in modern football leave that choice open for the quarterback to make on the fly. If he sees an opening to run, he can simply tuck the ball away and take off. Or he can find the open receiver and let it fly. With so much information to process in such a short amount of time, it's no wonder that finding good quarterbacks who can succeed at the NFL level is a tremendous challenge.

Quarterbacks will spend a lot of time in practice going through drills that put their decision-making to the test. Throwing against a timer can effectively replicate the pressure that the quarterback will feel from the oncoming rush. There are also rapid-fire throwing drills where the quarterback has to pick out a receiver instantly and fire off a pass. For a young quarterback, experiencing as much time pressure as possible, both in practice and during games, will help to develop the ability to see the field and respond with the right pass before it's too late.

MAKING CONTESTED CATCHES AS A WIDE RECEIVER

Getting wide open is pretty rare in competitive football. It's fun for the receiver when it happens, but those kinds of plays are few and far between. And, when a receiver is wide open, catching the ball is pretty easy. Anyone who has found their way onto a football field as a receiver is going to be able to catch a wide-open pass without any trouble.

In most cases, receivers have to try to make their catches with a defender in close proximity. The defender may be physically hanging onto the receiver, or they might be closing in quickly. Whatever the case, it's this ability to catch the ball under pressure that helps a young receiver stand out from the rest. Knowing how to latch onto the ball and not let go, even taking a hit along the way, makes it possible to pick up tough yards and keep the chains moving.

The first key to making contested catches is to high-point the ball. That means going up to get the ball at the highest possible point as it comes down. Waiting for the ball to fall is a recipe for disaster. At least, that kind of approach from a receiver is going to lead to an incomplete pass knocked away by the defender. Even worse, it could be intercepted. Receivers should always try to work back toward the ball when possible, which shortens the distance the ball has to travel and makes it more likely the catch will be made.

It's also vital for receivers to have strong hands when making contested catches. The ball should be snatched out of the air and squeezed tightly. There will always be a hit coming soon after the catch, so holding on firmly is key to securing the completion and avoiding a fumble. As the catch is made, the ball should be brought in and put away into a running position. Even the strongest receiver will have trouble holding onto the ball for the duration of the play if he keeps it out away from his body.

A good receiver will also learn how to use his body to keep the defender away from the ball, an advanced skill that can be thought of much like rebounding in basketball. Turning the body in such a way that the defender can't get into position to knock the ball away or intercept it is a high-level talent that will allow even more catches. Passing toward the sidelines usually means the receiver will put his body between the ball and the inside of the field. That effectively holds off the defense while the receiver can reach out over the out-of-bounds area and hopefully secure the ball.

A quarterback is naturally going to come to trust a receiver who is good at fighting for contested catches. The quarterback will know that the pass is unlikely to be intercepted when it is thrown toward a trusted receiver who will fight hard for position and snatch the ball out of the air. Being someone the quarterback can trust should be a goal for every young receiver hoping to see more time on the field and more targets during the course of a game.

HOW LINEBACKERS GET RID OF BLOCKERS

Linebacker is a challenging position to play. The physical demands alone are significant, as linebackers must be strong enough to deal with linemen while also being fast enough to keep up with running backs and receivers. And the physical requirements are only part of the job. A great linebacker is also the brains of the defense, acting as the leader on the field and helping everyone else get where they need to go. Just like it's hard to have a good offense without a quality quarterback, it's nearly impossible to put together a good defense without a reliable linebacker at the heart of it all.

For an offense, it's important to account for the linebackers when designing a play. These are the players who are most likely to make a tackle, so figuring out how to take care of the linebackers and get them blocked is always a top priority. Knowing that they will always be a target of the offense, linebackers must figure out how to move blocks away so they can continue pursuing the ball carrier and bring him down.

Some of the skills involved in removing blockers sound very similar to those used throughout the rest of the game. Keeping the feet moving is a big one. Just like with so many other positions, taking short steps and always staying balanced and ready to move in any direction is part of what the linebacker has to be able to do. Likewise, linebackers should stay low as they move around the field. Maintaining that low stance will have them ready to explode and make a powerful hit and tackle when the time comes.

Linebackers should also be skilled at using their hands and arms to push blockers away, which takes both skill and tremendous strength. Blockers will want to get in close to the linebackers to tie them up and limit their movement. It only takes a short block to give a running back or wide receiver enough time to sprint by. So, linebackers need to anticipate blocks, get their arms up to fight those blockers away, and move toward where the ball is going.

For young players with aspirations of playing linebacker, it's a good idea to watch some of the best in the game and note how they always seem to be free and ready to run. The good ones never manage to get tied up in blocks, or at least, it doesn't happen very often. Any young linebacker who frequently gets stuck on blocks and struggles to make tackles needs to work on both technique and strategy to stay free as often as possible. With a linebacker running loose and no one able to lock him up on a block, it's going to be hard for whoever has the ball on offense to get away and gain yards down the field.

DEFENSIVE BACKS CHANGE GAMES WITH INTERCEPTION

There are many opportunities for a defensive back to influence the game. The first, of course, is to understand how to play tight coverage on receivers. When a defensive back is always up close to a receiver, it makes life pretty tricky for the quarterback to find any success in the air.

Just as importantly, defensive backs need to be great tacklers in the run game. Linebackers won't be able to make all the plays, and it's often the defensive backs who need to come up to support the run defense and bring down the ball carrier. If a young player wants to make an impact on defense from the back of the field, knowing how to tackle properly—and consistently—will go a long way.

There is no doubt that making an interception is the biggest way that a defensive back can change the course of a game. An interception on the opponent's side of the field can set up the offense for an easy score. Even better, an interception when backed up close to the goal line can prevent the other team from cashing in on a long drive. Turnovers often decide the winners of football games, and interceptions specifically are huge plays that can swing momentum and determine who comes out on top.

Knowing the importance of getting interceptions, a young defensive player needs to develop skills that will help them take the ball away as often as possible. One of those skills is learning how to read the quarterback. It's much easier to make a pick, after all, if the defensive back has an understanding of where the ball might be thrown. By reading the quarterback's body language and eyes, it's possible to see into the future and start to move in the right direction even before the pass is made.

For example, if the quarterback has his shoulders open to the left side of the field, it's unlikely that the ball is going to the right. When the defensive back spots the quarterback in that kind of open stance, he can start to drift to the left side of the field in the hopes of making a big play. This kind of technique doesn't always pay off, of course, but it only takes one interception to change the course of the game in a new direction.

Seeing the quarterback's eyes from the secondary might sound kind of difficult, but it's easier than it seems because the quarterback's helmet gives away where he is looking. As the quarterback turns his head to go through reads, the defensive back can spot this movement. Just as when watching the shoulders, it's possible to respond to the movement of the eyes and adjust coverage accordingly. This technique is particularly effective for a free safety who isn't responsible for one specific receiver. He can watch the play develop, see where the quarterback is looking, and get a head start on hopefully picking off the pass.

THE LASER FOCUS OF A KICKER

A good kicker is essential to the success of a football team. It's awfully hard to win games when too many kicks are missed, after all. Whether they are field goals or extra points, knocking those kicks through the uprights as often as possible is a valuable skill that simply can't be overlooked when building a team.

There are several skills required to be a good kicker, starting, obviously, with the ability to kick the ball far and straight. Often, kickers will come to football from other sports, specifically soccer. A young soccer player who wants to get involved in more sports might consider joining the football team to apply his skills in a new area. While the technical skill of kicking the ball is critical, that alone will not be enough to thrive in this role.

The mental game is just as important when it comes to kicking a football. By definition, kickers are on the field during some of the most intense, pressure-filled moments of the game. The opportunity to score points is right in front of the team, but it takes a good kick to actually put the points on the board. Steady nerves and great focus are extremely important. If the kicker gets distracted by the pressure and is overcome with nervousness, even the best technical skills in the world won't make the ball go through the uprights.

One way for a kicker to develop focus is simply through experience. As more and more pressure situations are faced, the kicker will get increasingly comfortable with performing when it matters most. Young kickers might go through some tough moments where they miss important kicks and let down the team, but the key thing is that they come back stronger for the next time.

It also helps to learn how to focus only on what matters in the moment, which is executing the technical side of the kick. Where the plant foot will be placed, how the leg is going to swing through the ball, and where the kick should be aimed, based on wind and other factors, are the things that matter and should be the focus of the kicker as he prepares to take the field. All of the other stuff that can get in the way mentally, like thinking about the crowd or how many people will be disappointed if the kick is missed, is just a distraction. Great kickers block out everything else, stay committed to the process of kicking the ball, and knock it through more times than not.

CHAPTER SIX: DEVELOPING FITNESS & AGILITY

Football is extremely demanding from a physical perspective. There is just no way around it. This book will discuss the mental side of football in the next chapter, and while that is important, it all begins with physical ability. Having the fitness and agility necessary to keep up with the other players on the field is a starting point. From there, a young player can develop other valuable traits, such as an understanding of the mental game and proper technique in various positions.

Perhaps no sport demands more of its players than football. There is a need to check all of the athletic boxes to stay on the field and perform at a high level. It's necessary to be strong, of course. However, flexibility is also key to avoiding injuries, and speed is required to keep up with the rest of the players on the opposing team. A player with a glaring weakness in any physical category will quickly be exploited, and likely won't earn much playing time from the coach.

For young players, focusing on developing their bodies physically is an integral part of growing in the game and reaching their goals, which must be done intelligently and safely. Working with a coach or trainer who can provide a workout plan is one of the best ways to get in football shape while staying healthy throughout the journey.

STRENGTH TRAINING IS ESSENTIAL ON THE GRIDIRON

Being strong on the football field is really the only way to keep up in this game. Weaker players will be easily pushed off of blocks and knocked down during the course of play. It doesn't matter if a player is on offense or defense; strength is a prerequisite. As long as it doesn't come at the expense of speed, being strong is something that will always serve a football player well.

Strength is vital throughout the entire body, but it's particularly critical to be strong in the lower half. Exercises like squats and deadlifts build powerful legs that can withstand the pressure of pushing against another player. Imagine the battle that takes place at the line of scrimmage on each play. Sure, the players are fighting with their hands, but the real battle is taking place below the waist. Players with strong legs can dig in, push hard against the opponent, and win some ground.

On the other hand, a player with a weak lower body will have almost no chance to hold up, even if they have strong arms and shoulders. The legs are the foundation, and the rest crumbles if that foundation isn't strong enough to get the job done. The expression "never skip leg day" refers to always working the lower half of the body hard in the gym, and it applies directly to success on the football field.

A strategy should be considered when developing a plan to strengthen the lower body of a football player. Most of the work that goes into gaining large volumes of muscle needs to happen in the offseason. During that time, the player won't have to go through difficult practices or games, so they can afford to be sore in between gym sessions. That kind of soreness would be a problem during the season, but it's okay when the only thing on the schedule is more workouts.

That doesn't mean the working out stops when the season starts, however. Nothing could be further from the truth. Football players always need to be working out on a regular schedule, but shifting into maintenance mode during the season is also important. That means the players won't be trying to gain muscle so much as maintain the muscle they have already built. Maintenance lifting is lighter and less intense, but no less important.

SPEED WORK CAN'T BE OVERLOOKED

Football players are fast. That's an obvious statement for guys like running backs and wide receivers, but the speed of everyone on the field may surprise some fans. Even the big men who play in the middle of the field and don't have to sprint very often are quick on their feet. It's a game about speed as well as strength, and the team in any given game that is faster than the other will have a considerable edge.

There are several types of speed relevant in football. The first is flat-out sprint speed, the kind that is demonstrated by a wide receiver going out to catch a deep pass. He is simply sprinting down the sideline and trying to get past the defender using nothing more than sheer speed. Not everyone on the field has this type of speed, of course, and it's always amazing to see when a fast player can just blow by everyone else to get open.

Sprint speed is valuable, but another type of speed that matters in football might be more accurately described as quickness, which is the ability to move suddenly in one direction, only to switch up and move quickly in the other direction. It's also about picking up the feet quickly and then putting them back down again to get the body positioned just right. For linemen, this is what they need to do. They aren't often sprinting, but they do move their feet constantly to adjust their positioning and be in the right spot to make a key block.

Football players can improve their speed in several ways. First, for those who need to be sprinting down the sideline, like wide receivers and cornerbacks, maintaining a lean body is crucial. Additional size will slow a player down, so being as fit and muscular as possible is important. It's also essential to train for sprint speed by working on running mechanics. In many ways, players who want to be fast runners on the football field need to train like track athletes. In fact, many great football players have excelled in track events.

Ladder drills and other activities that focus on short-area quickness are great for everyone on a football team. This kind of work allows players to get better at those short, choppy, fast steps that make it easier to get in position to make a block, or to get around a block on the way to the ball carrier. A football player with slow feet will always be at a disadvantage and struggle to make an impact on the game. Even simple warm-ups, such as high knee jogging and side shuffles, can help refine footwork and prepare a player to be as sharp and quick as possible on the field.

BUILDING THE ENDURANCE TO PLAY FOUR QUARTERS

Football games are long. Each play is physically demanding, and completing just one would challenge most people. So, how do the best players manage to get through four quarters without breaking down completely? They have to be in incredible shape.

Every player on the field must possess outstanding physical endurance. The type of endurance required will vary from position to position, but everyone must be in shape and ready to go the distance. If a player's performance starts to fade as the game wears on, the coach will likely move that player to the bench and bring in someone else: an important lesson for young players to learn early on. Excellent physical conditioning can lead to more playing time, which should be motivation enough to work hard and get ready for the season.

One factor that influences endurance on the field is a proper diet. Eating the right food is like putting the right fuel in a car. It allows it to reach its full potential and avoid a premature breakdown. Football players who are only eating junk food and thinking that their effort on the field will be enough to burn off that junk are in for an unpleasant surprise. Poor-quality food is going to always leave a player short of reaching his full potential.

Another element at play here is engaging in endurance training from time to time to increase cardio health and stamina. The kinds of training that are usually associated with football tend to be workouts that are short and intense. Those are fine, and certainly beneficial, but they shouldn't make up a player's entire workout routine. Other exercises that are focused on endurance over the long run also need to be included. That could be anything from distance running on a track to simply engaging in long practice sessions where the intensity is maintained at a high level the whole time.

There is a mental component to endurance in a game that also needs to be respected. No matter how fit the players are, they will gradually wear down as the game progresses. That's just how humans work. But if the players on one team believe they are in better shape than the other team, they might have a mental edge in the fourth quarter. In fact, many teams are in the habit of having everyone on the team put up four fingers at the end of the third quarter as something of a rallying cry. The idea is that they are ready to play hard through all four quarters to win the game. Believing in their fitness level might be nearly as important as the actual fitness itself.

FLEXIBILITY IS OFTEN OVERLOOKED BY FOOTBALL PLAYERS

Football is not the first sport that comes to mind when talking about flexibility. Perhaps gymnastics would be high on that list. Most people don't picture someone who is particularly flexible when imagining the average football player. Flexibility is crucial in this game for several reasons.

The first is being able to make plays in awkward positions. Rarely in a football game is the situation that a player faces perfectly clean. It's not usually a case of being able just to run up and make a nice, easy tackle with no one in the way. Instead, there is typically another blocker to deal with, or maybe a whole mess of people that need to be navigated. Flexibility is critical in these situations. Being able to contort the body in different ways to grab onto a runner or to get away from a tackler is a skill that is often called upon.

Another way flexibility can pay off on the football field is through injury prevention. Football is a physically demanding game, and many players end up on the sideline with one type of injury or another. Steering clear of those injuries has something to do with luck, but it's also a matter of being flexible enough to have your body twist and turn without getting hurt. Specifically, flexibility in the leg muscles can avoid the kinds of strains and sprains that can lead to missing weeks at a time.

Perhaps not surprisingly, stretching is an excellent way to improve flexibility. In fact, it's virtually the only way to make it happen. Stretching is a great idea for all football players because as players get bigger in the weight room, they also tend to get tighter. Stretching can combat that tightness and help the player stay loose and ready to perform at their highest possible level.

Stretching should be a regular habit for any serious football player. Instead of viewing stretching as something that can be done in warm-ups, it should be seen as its own workout. Using a stretching routine at the end of a weightlifting session or after doing cardio is a great way to stay loose and be ready for the demands of practice or a game.

A young football player who wants to be as flexible as possible would be smart to start by focusing on the hamstrings. Just a few simple toe-touches can help loosen up the hamstrings gradually, especially when they are already warmed up after running. Having flexibility in the upper body is also important, so targeting the shoulders and other major areas around the chest and back will help.

TRAINING HAPPENS IN THE OFFSEASON

One of the biggest mistakes that young football players make is thinking that they can get in shape during training camp for the upcoming football season. It just doesn't work that way. Any player who shows up to training camp out of shape and not prepared to get to work won't have a good chance of making the team. That player may end up injured early on, or they might struggle to keep up with the other players who have been working hard for months to get ready for this moment.

There really isn't any offseason in football. Sure, there are times when games aren't being played, but that doesn't mean the work can stop. To a dedicated football player, any time when the season isn't technically in session is just an opportunity to be getting ready for the next season. Physical fitness, as has already been covered in this chapter, is just too important to take for granted by being lazy during the other months of the year when games or practices aren't scheduled.

The average young football player may have to do a lot of solo, individual work to get ready for the season. There might not be teammates available to work with or coaches to help put the player through drills. Taking the initiative to work out alone is necessary. In fact, that kind of drive can then carry over into the season, as the player learns how to take ownership of their own performance and not rely on others to move them forward.

It is worth noting that the same level of intensity can't be maintained for all twelve months of the year. A player trying to go all-out for the entire year will burn out and probably wind up injured. So, it's essential to have a strategic approach to adjusting the intensity of training throughout the year to achieve optimal results.

One effective way to approach training is to have a period of rest immediately after the season is over, allowing for both mental and physical recovery. After approximately two to three weeks of just light workouts, it may be time to transition into a complete offseason program that aims to build strength, grow muscle, and improve the player in every way. That type of intensive program can last for much of the offseason, but it shouldn't go all the way up to the start of training camp. Instead, there should be another recovery period before training camp begins. The recovery period will allow the player to address any nagging injuries from training and to regain full strength before competing for a role on the team.

With the right approach, a player can enter every season in excellent physical shape, which will make football more enjoyable and increase the likelihood of success in their chosen position. For a whole team, establishing an expectation that players arrive at training camp in shape and ready to go can make a huge difference. Instead of trying to get everyone up to speed and into playing shape, the team can work on installing plays, learning strategies, and coming together as a unit.

CHAPTER SEVEN: MASTERING THE MENTAL GAME

People who don't know a lot about football are often surprised to learn just how much of it is mental. These people picture football players as huge people who are packed with muscle and run around a field, hitting other players as hard as they can. That's how the game is played, but that reality doesn't tell the whole story. Behind those loud, violent collisions, the game is highly strategic, and it's the players who possess both physical abilities and mental skills that thrive, ultimately making teams and lifting trophies.

Whether a player is on offense or defense, there is a lot to know about strategy. With eleven players on both sides of the ball, there are nearly countless different ways that plays can be designed and run. There are a few rules in place that limit how plays are executed, but for the most part, offensive and defensive coordinators can be creative and find ways to trick the opposing side. While players don't have to be as knowledgeable as coaches in terms of how plays are created, they do need to understand the basics of what is done with the ball.

Strategy and play design are only part of the story when it comes to the mental game. It's also important to have confidence, understand how to be part of a team, and so much more. This chapter will dive into the specifics of the mental game of football so a young player can sharpen their mind and make it as strong as their body has become.

KNOWING HOW TO STUDY FOOTBALL FILM

When first getting started in competitive football, a player watching game film might feel like they are just watching a replay of the game. They might sit back, enjoy the show, and not really think much about it. That's not going to lead to any useful results, however. Watching game film to learn more about how the game works and how a player can improve is an active, involved process.

What the player is going to watch for depends entirely on what position they play on the field. Are they on offense or defense? For an offensive player, it's important to watch the tendencies of the defense. How do the defensive players tend to line up before the snap? Do they do anything to disguise the plays they are going to use? Perhaps they line up one way to make it look like they are going to be in a man defense, only to switch it up right before the snap and drop into a zone. The offense can also learn things like what the defense likes to do before they blitz, and whether they usually bring a rusher from the weak side or strong side of the line.

Every player on the offense, regardless of position, can benefit from this knowledge. For a lineman, knowing how the blitz tendencies work will help inform how the line shifts to pick up rushers and not leave the quarterback wide open to get hit. For a receiver, knowing when the blitz is coming, for example, helps them adjust their route and try to get open quickly for a short pass rather than going deep. It truly doesn't matter what the position is.

Everybody needs to have as much knowledge and information on their side as possible.

The story is much the same for defensive players, but only in reverse. On the defense, it's essential to understand the tendencies of the offense, starting with the quarterback. What does he usually do when certain formations are used? Does he like to throw to the tight end when one is on the field, or does he prefer hitting the receivers? Also, is this quarterback mobile enough to be considered a running threat, or is he sure to stay in the pocket all day long?

A defense will also want to learn during a film session which players on the other team they need to watch out for. It might be that an upcoming opponent has a particularly fast wide receiver who will require extra coverage from the safety. Or it might be the running back who appears to be the best player on the team. Film sessions are great for scouting, so the team isn't unprepared on gameday.

Despite having said so much about film sessions already, the most important part of watching film still hasn't been mentioned. That's the piece of the puzzle that involves a player watching his own performance from the last game. It can be hard to do, in some cases, as it might mean reliving plays that were frustrating or disappointing in some way. But that's actually the point. Young football players need to acknowledge their mistakes, take responsibility for them, and learn how to improve their performance. It's through these tough sessions that actual growth is made, and a player can really advance to the next level over time.

For one player, watching film of missed tackles might teach them that they are coming in too high and hitting the ball carrier in a position that doesn't lead to a good tackle. For a quarterback, it might mean watching film of an interception over and over again to determine what they should have seen on the play and what they missed. For players of every position, there is usually more to learn from mistakes than successes, so film study isn't always fun, but it is critical to development.

BUILDING CONFIDENCE ON THE FIELD

While football is perhaps the ultimate team sport, each play within the game is made up of moments where individual players must step up and get the job done. A single, individual mistake at the wrong time, like a missed assignment by a defensive back, can easily change the outcome of a game.

Knowing the importance that an individual play can have, it's easy for players, especially young players, to doubt themselves. Confidence is crucial in football, as it helps players to make the right moves and position themselves effectively on the field. A player who is full of doubt may wind up being too cautious in a big moment, allowing the play to unfold without them getting into position and making the right move at the right time.

Building confidence in anything is always tricky. It can't be faked, after all. Success is usually required for confidence to build, but in the absence of confidence, it's hard to find that success. A good way for a young football player to develop their confidence is to be as prepared as possible before a game, which aligns with the point about the value of film study. Reviewing tape from games and understanding how plays work in great detail will help the player feel confident about their approach. Even if they haven't had a ton of success on the field just yet, preparation can be an excellent substitute for experience.

Get as many reps as possible at whatever position is going to be played. For example, a running back should have as much experience in practice as possible, taking handoffs from the quarterback and putting the ball away in a good position before impact from a tackler. Doing this over and over again builds confidence, even if there are no stakes in practice. There will still be some nerves on the field for a game, of course, but all those reps during practice will give the player something to fall back on mentally.

Players within a team can also help each other with confidence. It's productive to lift teammates up by telling them they are doing a great job and helping the team to new heights. Positive affirmations go a long way toward boosting confidence, whether it is coming from teammates or coaches. Sometimes, the culture of football can become a little negative, with competitive players criticizing each other for mistakes they have made. That doesn't really help anyone, however. It's far better to be positive and encouraging, pushing each other forward and making the unit as a whole stronger. Even a couple of small compliments per day will gradually make a player feel like they deserve their spot on the team.

PLAY RECOGNITION: WILL IT BE A RUN OR A PASS?

One of the fundamental skills for every young football player to develop is learning how to differentiate between a run and a pass. The responsibilities of every player on defense will change based on the type of play being used by the offense. On a pass, the defensive backs need to drop back, while the linemen rush toward the quarterback. On a run, it's just the opposite; the linemen try to hold their ground and get off their blocks, while the defensive backs come up to support the linebackers in making a tackle.

There are several factors involved in learning how to quickly determine whether the play will be a run or a pass. First, there is the film study that we talked about earlier. Watching a lot of film intently is a great way to learn patterns and tendencies. When a particular group of players is on the field for the offense, what does that mean about whether they are likely to run or pass? Players who do a great job in the film room throughout the week are going to be better at diagnosing play selection when game day rolls around.

There are often clues before the snap of the ball that will help a defense decide if it's a run or a pass. For instance, the positioning of the running back in relation to the quarterback can indicate if he will be blocking or taking a handoff. Even subtle changes in the stances used by the offensive linemen can be a giveaway. If the linemen are on their toes, ready to charge forward, the defense will be on alert for a run. On the other hand, if those same linemen are on their heels and standing up a little taller, they are probably getting ready to pass block.

After the ball is snapped, eye discipline is key, which means avoiding distractions from the various tricks the offense uses to disguise the play. Specifically, linebackers need to keep their eyes in the right place to determine what is happening and then move to the right area. Again, the offensive linemen are one of the best keys. On a run, the linemen will start to charge forward when the ball is snapped, whereas they will stay back on a pass. Good linebackers will quickly read the movement of the line and then flow into position to stop the running back or break up a pass.

Knowing the down and distance situation is another piece of the puzzle. While there is no guarantee of what play will be called, the defense can use situational information to get an idea of what play will be used. Third and long is almost always a passing down, for example. Second and short might seem like a running down, but it's actually a common time for a deep pass, since the offense will have another chance on third down to run for it.

Finally, the time and score of the game also play into this equation. A team that has the lead late in the game is likely to call a lot of running plays to keep possession of the ball and run down the clock. On the other hand, a team that is behind will usually throw in the fourth quarter to hurry up and try to score before time runs out. Young football players can benefit from educating themselves on these various factors, so they aren't surprised by the plays that the offense uses to move the ball down the field.

THE ART OF EFFECTIVE LEADERSHIP IN FOOTBALL

Every football team needs good leaders. Sure, the coaches are going to provide leadership, but that's only part of it. Players need to be leaders too, and that role isn't limited to just the quarterback. Anyone on the team can be a leader, as long as they possess the characteristics of someone who will consistently take the team in a better direction, both in practice and during games.

The first trait of a true leader in football, and in every other aspect of life, is consistently doing the right things. A leader isn't someone who tells others to work hard during drills; it's the player who always works hard when doing their own drills. They don't take plays off, and they don't cut corners just to make things a little easier. In fact, they do just the opposite. They work even harder than required, going the extra mile to put in the effort needed to improve at this game.

Leading by example is really the only effective way to lead in football. A player who just yells at others to get the job done but then doesn't do it themselves will quickly be ignored. On the other hand, the player who tries their absolute best is going to automatically become a leader, even if they don't say a word. These kinds of internal team leaders don't wait for the coach to yell at them to start working; they have been working hard the whole time.

While it's not necessary for a good leader on a football team to be outspoken, it is important that a leader listens to the issues of others. They should be open to hearing what other players are struggling with so they can be supportive. That might mean giving them advice, or it could mean pointing them toward the right coach who can help with their struggles. Having a few leaders on the team who are working hard, always willing to listen, and reliably show up day after day can go a long way toward building a winning season.

Leadership should also extend beyond the field, which is particularly important for young football players who may need to see positive role models around them to stay out of trouble. Players on a youth football team who make good decisions, avoid associating with the wrong people, stay focused on their schoolwork, and take other steps to build a solid foundation in life will naturally become leaders for others to follow. While it's not necessarily tied to skill on the field, having at least a few of the team's best players also be good examples off the field can be very helpful.

BOUNCING BACK FROM INEVITABLE ADVERSITY

Adversity is a natural part of football and life. There will always be setbacks. Even the best players and the best teams are going to have bad days. Mistakes will be made, and losses will occur.

Success in this game isn't about being perfect, but it is about what happens immediately after a failure occurs.

Adversity can come in many forms, and the appropriate response will depend on what has happened. For example, during a game, a team might get a bad bounce that allows the other team to recover the ball. That's unfortunate, but there is no time to wallow in frustration. Teammates need to support one another, stay positive, and prepare for the next play. The game will just keep going, after all.

The same can be said for when an individual player makes a costly mistake. Maybe it's an open receiver dropping a sure touchdown pass. Or it could be a defensive back blowing an assignment and leaving the other team open to score. In these situations, the support of teammates is helpful, and the leadership discussed above becomes vital. A team leader can approach the player who made a mistake, offer support, and encourage them to keep going. It's always easier for individuals to bounce back from adversity when they feel the love of the team around them.

Another type of adversity in football is a painful loss in a close game. After battling for four quarters and coming up just a bit short, it's easy for the team as a whole to be let down. It's okay to feel those emotions for a little while and acknowledge the frustrations of the loss, but they can't linger for too long. After all, there is probably another game to play next week.

Good teams don't point fingers after a loss. They don't blame each other in the locker room, and they don't pin the loss on bad referees or bad luck. Instead, they take ownership of the situation and dive into the film of the game to spot their mistakes and learn how to get better next time. There is more to be learned from a loss than a win, as long as the team is willing to watch the film with an open mind and identify areas for improvement.

CHAPTER EIGHT: COMMUNICATION CREATES STRONG TEAMS

It's easy for communication to get lost in the shuffle in football. Young players are usually focused on developing various skills needed on the field, like strength and speed. Additionally, many young players focus on learning the game from a strategic standpoint, including watching film and understanding plays and formations, as discussed earlier in this book.

All of those things are important. However, they can be wasted mainly if proper communication skills aren't in place. Communicating effectively is like a superpower, both in football and in life. Knowing how to share a message with others in a way that is received quickly and accurately will improve outcomes across the board. Quality communication skills aren't something that people are born with. These skills are developed through consistent practice and repetition.

What does communication in football look like? Sometimes, it's an obvious form of communication, like the quarterback yelling out signals at the line of scrimmage just before the snap of the ball. Other times, it can be so subtle that it's nearly invisible. For instance, a defensive lineman might tap the leg of another lineman just before the snap to tell him to shift over slightly to gain an advantage.

It's already been established that football is a team game in every sense, and effective communication allows a team to come together and perform better than the sum of its parts. For a young football player looking for every possible edge to advance in the game, knowing how to communicate properly with teammates in practice and games is a valuable skill to possess.

USING ON-FIELD SIGNALS EFFECTIVELY

Football is a loud game. While there is plenty of talking on the field, it's not always possible to hear other players or coaches clearly. It's even more difficult because everyone is wearing a helmet that interferes somewhat with hearing, and no one can really read lips through a facemask. Additionally, one team may not want the other team to hear what they are saying, so shouting signals across the field isn't a great plan.

When it's all added up, the value of hand signals becomes obvious. Having a complete set of hand signals that everyone on the team understands, and that are foreign to the other team, helps players and coaches communicate without giving anything away. In most cases, both the offense and the defense will have various hand signals that enable them to change things on the fly and keep everyone on the same page.

For example, a quarterback will have a set of hand signals that he can use with his wide receivers at the line of scrimmage. The receivers are too far away to shout new instructions at the line, and the defense would be able to hear what is said. With hand signals, the receivers can quickly make adjustments, like changing to a different route, based on what the defense is showing. An audible is an example. The quarterback decides that the play called in the huddle isn't going to work, so an audible is called, and hand signals are used to share the new play with everyone.

This type of communication works the same way on the defensive side of the ball; however, it's usually a linebacker who is in charge of sending the signals out. They might need to use a gesture to make an adjustment to the type of defense being played, or to call a blitz if the offensive setup looks vulnerable. The moments before the snap of the ball tend to be a flurry of hand signal activity on both sides until the play actually starts.

For a young player, the important thing is to study hand signals regularly to know exactly what they all mean. Understanding the signals should be second nature once training camp is over and the games begin. It doesn't matter if a player is responsible for giving signals or just receiving them; having a detailed understanding of the signs is just as important as knowing the playbook.

DELIVERING INSTRUCTIONS IN THE HUDDLE

It can help to think of a huddle as the calm before the storm. Once a football play begins, the action on the field is just short of complete chaos. Fortunately, there is time before the play starts to gather in a huddle with the rest of the team and quickly discuss the plan. It's well known that the offense needs to huddle up, in most cases, before starting a play, but it is common for the defense to do the same. Even if the defense doesn't use a formal huddle, some type of communication will still be taking place, with players generally gathering around to get on the same page.

The player with the most huddle-related responsibilities on the field is, of course, the quarterback. On offense, the quarterback takes control of the huddle and delivers the instructions for the upcoming play. For a young player at the quarterback position, learning how to use a loud, commanding voice in the huddle is essential. The play call needs to be spoken with authority and pronounced clearly so that everyone knows what's going on. If it's hard for the rest of the team to hear the instructions or they misunderstand what was said, the play is doomed to fail.

Eye contact is also important during a huddle. The quarterback should look directly into the eyes of his teammates to see that they are receiving the message and understanding it. Any confusion can be read on their faces, and the instructions can be repeated for clarity. It's helpful for the offense to get into the huddle quickly, allowing them plenty of time to make the play call and get up to the line with time to spare before the play clock runs out.

On the defensive side of the ball, it's usually the middle linebacker who plays the role of "quarterback." He will be responsible for making the play calls and getting everyone in the right position prior to the snap. That same linebacker should be making eye contact with others on the defense so he can shift them into the right spots if they are out of place. There won't be any time to get things organized after the play starts, so the huddle and the moments after the huddle are the last chances to dial in the defense and be ready for whatever the offense has in store.

There is a lot of practical information that needs to be shared quickly in the huddle. The play call needs to come in from the sidelines and then be relayed to everyone so they can get in position and start the next play. But that's not the only function of a huddle. It's also a great time to reset from the previous play, take a breath, and support everyone else on the team. If a player made a mistake on the last play, everyone else in the huddle can "pick them up" and offer words of encouragement. Or, if there was a great play, a moment of congratulations can be shared while the new play is coming in. A team with a positive culture in place will use the huddle as a proactive time to make sure they are staying together and still working toward the same goal.

EVERY PLAYER NEEDS TO FILL A ROLE

Football only works when every player on the field is performing their role. No one player can do everything, and it takes all eleven being unified and organized to make any progress. Of course, for each player to perform their role properly, they need to understand what that role is and how it relates to the roles of others. Young football players need to learn about the various roles within a team and how they come together like a jigsaw puzzle.

The offensive line can serve as a good example of how communication and playing roles come together to produce great results. The offensive line is a group of five players that have two basic functions: to protect the quarterback on pass plays, and to make room for the running back on running plays. Those goals are simple, but if the individual linemen don't understand their roles, the outcome will not be what is desired or expected.

For example, two offensive linemen might be given the job of double-teaming a terrific rusher on the defense. That can be a great plan, but only if the two linemen performing the double team know their assignment and communicate effectively with one another. If neither player knows their role, in other words, the whole plan falls apart. This same line of thinking can apply to line shifts. Some plays will call for the entire line to shift in one direction or the other. Again, this technique only works when all roles are filled, and communication is clear.

Playing the right roles on the field starts with communication, but that's certainly not where it ends. There is also an element of buying into the plan that comes into play. Every player needs to commit fully to his role and not try to do his own thing independently. For instance, imagine a receiver who is supposed to run a specific route as a distraction on a given play, so someone else can get open. If that receiver doesn't take his role seriously, he might not run very hard as the decoy, immediately indicating to the defense that he isn't a serious threat. Even though the ball was never going to go to that receiver, he could ruin the entire play by not committing to his role as a decoy.

The best teams are those that not only have talent but also have a collection of players who are all willing to commit fully to their assigned roles. That role might not be exactly what they wanted it to be, but those are decisions for the coaches to make. Once given an assignment, it's up to the individual player to execute that assignment for the greater good of the team.

SUPPORTING TEAMMATES ON THE FIELD

Emotions run high in football. Whether it's a game that isn't going well, a long, difficult practice, or just a big mistake that causes tempers to flare, emotion is part of the game. Football wouldn't be what it is without those emotions, so they certainly don't need to be removed entirely.

They do need to be controlled, however. A good team will have players who know how to control their emotions and channel them toward productive performance. When emotions get the better of a player or team, it is almost impossible to achieve positive results.

Here again is where we see the value of teamwork and communication in football. It's important to support teammates while on the field, but it needs to be done correctly. Young players might not understand how to support their teammates in a productive way, but with a little practice, it's possible to develop this valuable skill.

The first key to supporting teammates on the field is to be relentlessly positive. It's not the time for negativity or criticism. Even if a player thinks another player should do something differently, it is not the time for those kinds of comments on the field during the middle of a game. Instead, it should just be a simple "you got this," or something along those lines. Players should support one another on the field to help keep the emotion of the game from turning in the wrong direction.

Sometimes, it will be necessary for one player to step in and tell another player to calm down and get focused again. It can be more challenging than simply providing affirmations, and it may fall to a team captain to play this role. But it's extremely important. If one player is obviously getting frustrated and losing their cool, such as might happen after a big mistake or a string of bad plays in a row, someone else on the team can step in and help them calm down. It can still be done in a positive way, but it needs to be clear and direct.

It's also important to remember that teammates should never embarrass one another on the field. Likely, people are watching as the game is being played, so openly arguing in the middle of the field or pointing fingers at one another isn't appropriate. If those difficult discussions are necessary to work things out, they should happen in private and behind closed doors. While out on the field, the tone of the team as a whole should be supportive and helpful. Everyone should be in it together, win or lose.

BONDING AWAY FROM THE GRIDIRON

If communication between members of a football team is limited to the field itself, that team will struggle to build a true bond that carries it through the toughest moments of a season. It's hard to develop natural, easy communication when players only spend time together on the field. If possible, it's best if players spend at least some of their time together off the field, as well. Those hours spent bonding when doing anything other than football can actually be extremely valuable during practice and game situations.

Sometimes, this bonding occurs during times related to football activities, but not while playing the game. Bus rides or hanging out in the locker room are two examples. There is a bunch of time that will inevitably be spent together as part of a team, and it all helps grow the bond. If this is a team associated with a school, the players will likely have classes together, eat lunch with each other, and engage in other activities together.

It's also a good idea for the coaches to plan team events. Something like a team bowling night or volunteering for a community service is an excellent opportunity to come together. Similarly, simple things like gathering at someone's house to play video games and relax for a while are also enjoyable. Or it could be getting together on a Sunday to watch an NFL game. The options are virtually endless, but the goal is always the same. To develop the kind of supportive, welcoming family environment that makes everyone feel connected and invested in the success of the team as a whole.

There's more to team bonding activities than just serving the goal of better communication. It's also simply a way to make the experience of being on a football team more enjoyable. For young players, getting to know teammates and building friendships with them is a massive part of what makes the journey worthwhile. In the long run, it's really those things that make football worth playing. The bond with teammates tends to last long beyond the end of the last game. Players will likely forget the results of certain games or the statistics they accumulated in their careers. However, they will remember the people with whom they did those things along the way.

CHAPTER NINE: DRILLS & ROUTINES TO BUILD SKILLS

There is no debating the thrill of playing in a football game. The excitement is off the charts, and it's what this sport is all about. Getting to take the field under the lights and go to battle with teammates against the opposition is an amazing challenge and opportunity.

It only comes through hard work and dedication to the game. If a young player doesn't work hard at football and just wants to come out and play in the games, they likely won't see the field (or even make the team). Getting the chance to line up on the field and be in the middle of the action is something that is earned, not given.

Young players can benefit greatly from understanding the value and importance of drills and practice routines. They can be used throughout the year to improve and develop the skills that coaches want to see. Sure, these drills might not always be exciting. In fact, they can be downright boring. But that's simply part of the work that has to be done to get better at the game.

Most of the time, no one will be watching as these drills are performed. No one will be there to offer congratulations or to provide encouragement to keep going. It's in these moments that the kind of character and toughness required in football are truly developed. In addition to developing a set of diverse skills, the player is creating the determination to persevere, to keep pushing forward, and to learn how to overcome challenges to emerge stronger on the other side. The mental benefits of drill work and practice routines are almost certainly just as valuable as what is gained physically from these exercises.

SOLO DRILLS ARE GREAT FOR THE OFFSEASON

The core of building football skills lies in performing solo drills. It might be obvious, but the great thing about solo drills is that no one else is needed. They can be performed pretty much anywhere, anytime. They are great in the offseason when a player wants to develop particular skills outside of the structured practice environment, but they can also be used during the season. For virtually any skill needed on a football field, there is a solo drill that is applicable.

For players on the offensive side, two specific categories of solo drills tend to be the most useful: ball handling and footwork. Of course, ball handling really only applies to some of the players on the offense, but everyone needs good footwork. So, doing things like running through cone layouts or chopping quick steps back and forth through a ladder serve as excellent solo drills. For a player who handles the ball, such as a running back, blending ball handling and ladder work is an excellent simulation of what will be needed when game time finally arrives.

Quarterbacks can even do solo throwing drills to work on their accuracy. With a bucket of footballs and an open field, it's easy enough to set up a target and start working on hitting the spot. Accurate throws are always important, and even if the quarterback isn't dealing with a field full of defenders to navigate, this work is still worthwhile. The more accurate a quarterback can be when throwing to stationary targets, the more likely he will be to hit his actual receivers when they are being covered tightly by a defensive back.

Are linemen out of luck when it comes to solo drills? Definitely not. As mentioned above, ladder work and other footwork drills are appropriate for every player on the field. Additionally, linemen can practice getting into a balanced stance repeatedly and coming out of that stance to engage a block. Finding a sled to push is often easy enough, so solo sled work can be done to build muscle and optimize technique. This type of practice can benefit players on both sides of the line.

Consistency is the name of the game with solo drills. It's best to do them regularly, throughout the year, rather than only in intense bursts from time to time. For example, consider a player who does ten minutes of solo drills every day for a month. That player has done 300 total minutes of drills in that month. By comparison, another player has also done 300 minutes of work but divided into just three sessions of 100 minutes each. Who has improved more? Almost certainly the player who did drills every day; that consistent repetition can't be replicated with long sessions that only happen every once in a while. The players who get the most out of solo drills are those who come back to them day after day for short periods of intense, focused effort.

PARTNER DRILLS CAN BUILD IMPORTANT SKILLS

There is sure to be plenty of solo work involved in developing the kinds of skills needed to thrive on a football field. It's a team sport at the core, so working together with others is always a great way to improve. Young players who want to build as many skills as possible that will translate to success during actual game action should find ways to work together with teammates. That will happen during formal practices, of course, but it can also be scheduled into the offseason and non-practice days.

Partner drills are great because they are simple and require only one other person to perform. It's probably not practical to bring together a bunch of different teammates to work on skills, but connecting with just one other player is easy. In addition to the fact that partner drills will make it simple to work on skills that are hard to master alone, there is extra motivation that can be drawn from scheduling this kind of session. The accountability that comes from having a partner should make everyone work harder and stay more focused in the end.

The classic partnership for two-person drills in football is a quarterback and a receiver. Perhaps more than any other duo on the field, players at these two positions need to be on the same page play after play. Any miscommunication or poor timing between a quarterback and a receiver will result in a failed pass at best, and an interception at worst. Going through routes with the quarterback throwing pass after pass will develop chemistry between the two players that will pay off at game time. The quarterback will learn how his receiver runs routes, how quickly he can change directions, and how fast he is when sprinting down the field. It takes a lot of reps, but the two can come to work as one after enough time.

A quarterback is not the only player that a receiver can work with during partner drills, however. Pairing up with a cornerback to practice running routes while being covered is another great exercise. The receiver will be able to work on getting free from coverage, while the cornerback can work on his footwork and quickness to stay right on the receiver's hip. These players, who are typically opponents on the field, can work together during practice sessions to improve each player's skills.

This same concept can apply to linemen. An offensive lineman can get together with a defensive lineman to practice one-on-one drills at any time. These drills are simple. It's just lining up across from each other and going to battle. Working on hand-fighting and football is far more productive when there is an actual person on the other side of the line waiting to be engaged. Linemen can also benefit from solo drills, but it's really in these partner drills where meaningful progress is made, and practice starts to feel more like an actual game situation.

It's a good idea for young football players to develop relationships with multiple practice partners at various positions. That way, it's easy to find someone who is available when the time comes to work on some drills. These partnerships help to form bonds that will be valuable during the season and beyond. There's nothing wrong with having one favorite practice drill partner, but getting together with various other players on the team from time to time can help develop even more skills and turn any player into a leader.

TEAM DRILLS ARE THE BEST PREPARATION FOR GAME ACTION

There is a lot to love about solo and partner drills, as has been highlighted in the previous two sections. Those types of practices should absolutely be included in the training program of any serious young player. With that said, full team drills are critical to the success of the entire unit, so working together with all eleven players on the field at once is something that has to happen as often as possible.

Solo and partner drills are where valuable individual skills are developed. Team drills, on the other hand, are where players learn how to use the skills they have built within the context of the offense or defense as a whole. A football team of eleven players working individually on the field will never get the job done, no matter how skilled those players may be. It's only when the unit is cohesive and connected that the results will start to show through.

Sometimes, young players struggle to see how the work they are doing on the field benefits the team, especially when they aren't getting the ball on a given play. Team drills can help to clarify the value of everyone's role. Wide receivers can be a perfect example of this concept. There are many plays where a receiver isn't going to be targeted with the ball, so it would be tempting for a player, especially a young player, to take those plays "off" and not really run hard. However, during team drills, the value of running good routes, even when the ball won't be coming, can be seen. Running a good route will hold the attention of the corner, and maybe even a safety, opening up space for the player who will have the ball.

This same concept applies to the work done by a defensive tackle. Suppose the goal of the defensive play is to allow a linebacker to rush the quarterback freely. In that case, the defensive tackle needs to lock up a couple of offensive linemen. If the tackle can command the attention of the offensive line by making a push, the linebacker should have plenty of space available to shoot the gap and go for a sack. When these little details become obvious during team drills, every player on the field will understand the value they bring in all situations.

Doing situational work is something else that can only really occur during team drills. The way a team approaches each play is dictated by the game situation, as a strategy that makes sense at one point in the game would be completely inappropriate at another time. For example, if the team is ahead by ten points late in the game, running down the clock will be the top priority. Working on drills that emphasize things like staying in bounds and snapping the ball with only a couple of seconds left on the play clock will help when these situations actually arise.

Perhaps the most important type of situational work is the two-minute drill. This drill simulates an end-of-game scenario in which the offense is behind by a few points and needs to work quickly to move the ball down the field. While a two-minute drill won't be necessary in every game—it might only come up a few times per season—it's essential to execute it properly to have a chance to turn a loss into a win.

Of course, when a team is working on a two-minute drill, both the offense and defense are getting valuable reps. For the offense, players will learn how to move quickly and set up for each play without committing penalties or getting out of position. On the defensive side, players will be forced to stay disciplined and keep the offense in front of them to avoid a big play and a quick score. There is a tremendous amount of pressure felt during a two-minute drill in a real game, but that pressure won't be so bad if the situation has been practiced countless times before.

SPECIAL TEAMS DRILLS CAN MAKE ALL THE DIFFERENCE

One of the biggest mistakes made by players and coaches in football is treating special teams like an afterthought. Some players see special teams as a minor, insignificant part of the game. In reality, nothing could be further from the truth. Kicking plays have a massive impact on the outcome of each game. The team that executes these plays properly will have a significant advantage over the opposition.

In addition to the team value of special teams, there is also the potential value of these units for individual players. If a given player is having a hard time getting on the field for offense or defense, special teams could be an opportunity to see some game action. Then, if good work is done on the special teams unit, the player may be given more opportunities at their offensive or defensive position.

Given the importance of special teams, it only makes sense that special teams drills should be completed regularly. Just like other areas of the game, special teams is an area that can benefit greatly from the use of drills, both on an individual and team basis. Executing special teams plays correctly is a matter of coordination in which everyone plays. So, team drills should always have a place in the daily practice plan.

For kickers and punters, there is nothing like repetition. Simply kicking the ball over and over again will develop skills and build the confidence needed to perform under pressure. If a place kicker sees the ball fly through the uprights time after time during practice drills, for example, kicking field goals during the game won't feel quite so intimidating. There will still be nerves, of course, but the completed repetitions will provide positive reinforcement and give the kicker the boost that is needed to get the job done when it really matters.

Individual kicking reps are helpful, without question, but special teams drills are really about learning how to coordinate with everyone else on the field. Take a punt as a perfect example. Yes, the punter needs to kick the ball high and far, but that's only one piece of the puzzle. For the punt play to be successful, both blocking and coverage also need to be excellent. The line needs to block the rushers to make sure the punter has time to get the ball out. The coverage players need to sprint down the field, getting off of their blocks and positioning themselves correctly to make sure the returner doesn't get far.

Every good football coach will incorporate special teams drills into practice regularly, but the effort of the individual players must be high if the work is going to pay off. There should be no going through the motions during special teams practice. Players shouldn't view this as a break or downtime between other parts of the practice schedule. Sure, special teams can be a bit tedious, but players will be happy they worked hard during drills when they get great results in a game and gain an edge over the opponent.

CONDITIONING DRILLS ARE A NECESSARY EVIL

It's no secret that conditioning drills are despised by most football players. It's not the fun part of the game. Going through conditioning is extremely demanding, as these drills are designed to be even harder than what will be experienced during gameplay. Since conditioning can be so unpleasant, it's tempting for players to cut corners or to complain to coaches that they are working them too hard.

Like everything else in football, however, success comes down to who is willing to put in the effort. Given two teams that are relatively equal in football skill, the team that has truly embraced conditioning and has pushed itself to the limit long before game day is going to be in better shape and will likely own the fourth quarter. Not only will the better-conditioned team avoid physical breakdown, but they will also be more likely to avoid costly mistakes.

While conditioning drills might be difficult, they aren't complicated. The purpose of these drills, whether performed with a team or individually, is to replicate the specific physical demands experienced during a football game. Football is a game that is played in short bursts, over and over again, for four quarters. It's not about steady, long-term endurance, like would be required when running a marathon. Instead, football requires players to give their all for just a few seconds at a time, rest briefly between plays, and then repeat the process.

Given the nature of the game and the type of conditions that tend to be important on the gridiron, interval training should be the focus for young players. It starts with wind sprints. No, they aren't any fun to do, but they do closely mimic what happens on the field. Wind sprints can be performed alone or with a group of people. The structure of a wind sprint routine can vary wildly from one to the next, but the idea is always the same. There is a short, intense, and all-out sprint, followed by a brief recovery.

Here's an example of how wind sprints can be performed effectively on a football field. A player or players stand on the goal line at one end of the field to get ready for the first sprint. When the drill starts, the players sprint down the field until they reach the fifty-yard line (this distance can be adjusted as needed). Once at the fifty-yard line, players shut it down and start walking the rest of the distance to the other goal line. Once that goal line is reached, everyone turns around and sprints back out to midfield again.

Needless to say, these sprints are going to get difficult in a hurry. It's always important to keep safety in mind, so the structure of sprints should be turned down a bit if the weather is particularly hot. Also, there should always be plenty of water readily available so everyone can stay hydrated. Sprints are a classic, foundational piece of football conditioning, but it's also worthwhile to include other forms of cardio work, such as shuttle runs.

Of course, strength can't be overlooked in a football conditioning program. There will be plenty of time spent in the weight room, although that doesn't really fit into the category of "drills" covered in this section. For drills that build strength, players can engage in activities like pushing weighted sleds and flipping tires on the field. Not only are these activities great for building muscle, but they also mimic actions that will be used on the field during practices and games.

One important note to make about conditioning is that it is not punishment. A culture has developed around conditioning over the history of football—and many other sports—that positions it more as a form of punishment than anything else. Not working hard enough in practice, or messed up on a key play? Conditioning might be assigned. That's counterproductive, however. Conditioning is simply another part of preparing to play football well. Yes, it's hard, but it shouldn't be seen or used as a tool for teaching a lesson. When viewed in a positive, productive light, it will be easier to approach conditioning with the right attitude.

SCHEDULING RECOVERY INTO THE PROCESS

It would be easy to read through this chapter on football drills and come to the conclusion that it's necessary to work nonstop at this game. After all, if doing some drills is good, it would seem like even more drills would be better. And to be sure, working hard is a necessary part of improving at football, but there is a point where it starts to become counterproductive.

Recovery is a necessary part of any physical pursuit. It's critical to give the human body time to recover from any challenging activity, no matter what it may be. Whether it's a baseball pitcher who needs a few days of rest after pitching several innings, or a distance runner taking a break during marathon training, rest is a critical part of every sport.

The story is certainly the same in football, so young players need to learn how to strike the right balance. There should always be a goal in place to get as much as possible out of the body without going so far that injuries and fatigue become a major risk. As a general rule of thumb, it's okay to push harder in training during the off-season, as there are no games to be ready for on the weekend. However, once the season starts, players will want to back off, just a bit, on the intensity of their drills and conditioning work to make sure the tank is full for every game all season long.

There is an element of trial and error involved in finding the right volume of training for football drills. Not every player will respond the same way to different types of training and conditioning. For example, some players will struggle more to recover from a strength workout, while others will be wiped out from cardio conditioning. Each player needs to get to know their own body and adjust their training habits to find just the right balance.

It's also valuable to have a few training partners who can keep an eye on one another. If a workout partner notices that someone is looking a little tired or slow, he can say something and suggest that they take a day off. That kind of mutual support and feedback can go a long way toward optimizing the use of drills and positioning the player perfectly for a great season.

CONCLUSION

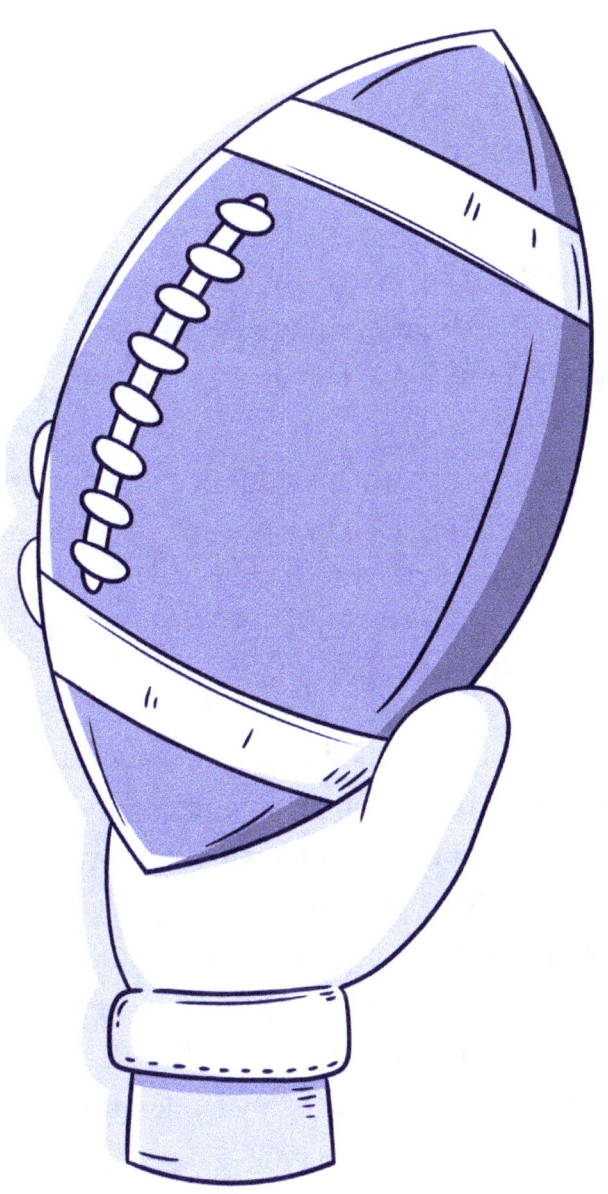

Football is much more than just a game. Sure, there is a scoreboard, and one side will be a winner at the end of each contest. But the sport is about so much more than wins and losses. At the risk of dipping into cliche territory, this is a game that prepares players for what they are going to encounter for the rest of their lives, far beyond the lights of the stadium. Young football players who become invested in the game and truly commit to becoming the best they can be will continue to reap the benefits of that hard work for a lifetime.

The football field can be seen as another type of classroom. In this case, however, rather than learning subjects like math and writing, young people learn valuable lessons in discipline, teamwork, and perseverance. Every obstacle encountered on the field is an opportunity to grow as a person. Every accomplishment is an opportunity to build more confidence and foster greater belief in what can be achieved in the future. Life is never easy, and neither is football. The two mirror each other closely, and thriving in one is likely to correlate with thriving in the other.

It's common for adults to notice a dramatic change in a young person who gets involved in football and becomes invested in the team environment and the pursuit of improvement. Where a young player may have previously been going down a negative path, their involvement in football can turn things around in an instant. It offers a positive force and a reason to grow and develop. It provides purpose and meaning. No matter how many touchdowns are scored or how many games are won, the impact of the game is sure to be far-reaching and powerful.

BECOMING A WELL-ROUNDED FOOTBALL PLAYER

If there is a single lesson that every young player should take away from this book, it's the importance of being well-rounded. It's easy to look at professional football players who have one specific, incredible skill and think that football is all about specialization. That's not really the case, especially for young players. Instead, learning how the game works as a whole, and trying as much of it as possible along the way, is the best path forward.

Being a well-rounded player doesn't mean just playing a lot of positions, although that could be part of it. Having as many different physical capabilities as possible is great, such as being a fast runner, a strong tackler, or a powerful thrower. To really be well-rounded, however, it's necessary to have just as much ability in the mental parts of the game as the physical components. A player who studies film carefully to understand offensive and defensive schemes, or to scout an upcoming team and understand who their players are and what they like to do, will be extremely valuable.

A part of this discussion also involves being someone that the coach can always count on to do the right thing. When someone is a well-rounded player, they get to practice on time, they always work hard without being told to do so, and they respect their teammates (more on that in a moment). These are the players that coaches love to have, and they are the people that others love to be around in life. In short, they aren't part of the problem, but rather, part of the solution.

Blending physical abilities with positive character traits is a powerful combination. When those two things come together, extraordinary things can happen on the field. A football player who works hard enough to be physically ready is dedicated and hard for the opposition to handle. Having just a few guys like this on a team can be a problem for the other side. When the whole team is full of players who fit this description, the other side hardly stands a chance.

APPROACHING THE GAME WITH HUMILITY & RESPECT

No one is bigger than the game of football. It doesn't matter how rich or famous a player becomes; the game is always bigger. Football goes on even after the legends of the NFL retire, as there are always new up-and-coming players ready to fill in the gaps and steal the headlines. However, a player doesn't have to reach the NFL level to understand this concept. Players at all levels need to remain humble and bring a respectful attitude to the field.

Part of this humility involves understanding that there is no such thing as a perfect player. Every single player, without exception, can improve. There is always something to work on and get better at. It could be a skill, like getting into a good stance or developing better footwork, or it could be a physical trait, like getting stronger. Whatever the case, no player is perfect, and the opportunity to improve is always waiting out there to be explored. When players understand that they can and should continuously be improving, there isn't the space available to develop a big ego and become too good to put in the hard work.

It can be hard for players to remain humble as they accumulate accolades and achievements. For example, if a player scores a few touchdowns early in the season and is being praised by everyone, it's easy to let the ego get a bit out of control. That's natural, and it's vital for the team to have a strong environment where everyone is just a piece of the puzzle, rather than being the star of the show. With good coaching and effective team leadership, it's possible to maintain a supportive and healthy environment that keeps everyone in the right mental state to continue improving.

Respecting the game and other players on the field is also a key piece of learning and growing in football. Respecting teammates is a good starting point, as no one gets anywhere in this game without great teammates. That respect should also extend to the players on the other teams, the officials, coaches, fans, and everyone else involved in making football happen. Being respectful means always treating others kindly, understanding that things don't always go as expected, and generally trying to contribute to creating a positive environment for others.

Being respectful in football is good simply because it is the right thing to do. In addition to acting considerately toward others, maintaining respect for the game at all times can also help players move forward and open up new opportunities. For example, if a high school football player wants to have a chance to play on a college team, being known as a respectful and hard worker will go a long way. Given the choice between two players with similar physical traits and capabilities, the more respectful, humble player is going to be preferred by a coach every single time.

USING GOALS TO DRIVE GROWTH

Getting better at football is not something that happens by accident. Just randomly working on various drills from time to time isn't really going to move the needle very far. As in every other part of life, getting better at football requires focus and a plan. Players who understand what they want to improve and how to achieve it will have a significantly better chance of reaching their desired goal.

The best goals are those that are small and within reach. For example, if a young player sets a goal to make the NFL someday, that's certainly aspirational—but it's not very motivating on a daily basis. It's just too far away and too big to really act on in a meaningful way. A much better way to approach goals would be to pick out three areas the player wants to improve over the next few weeks. These could be things like improving sprint speed, getting stronger in a certain lift in the gym, and getting a better understanding of how zone defense works.

At first, those might seem like small goals, but they can actually be transformative when accumulated over time. The player could spend time working on that first set of goals before moving on to another set of targets, and on and on. In this manner, continual improvement can add up and transform a young player into an impressive prospect. For each relatively small goal, some actions can be taken to get closer to the target. In the case of these examples, the player can do running drills to get faster, target the specific lift in the gym for the next workout cycle, and watch extra film focused on zone defense concepts.

Goals are easier to track when they are written down, and tangible steps are outlined to work toward those goals. They shouldn't just be stored mentally. They don't feel real until they are put out into the world somewhere. It's a good idea to have an accountability partner who is also working on goals and can come along on this journey. When goals are met, they can be momentarily celebrated while new ones are set.

The power of compound improvements can be challenging for young football players and young people in general to understand. But it's very real. Improving one specific skill in a very specific way often doesn't feel like it will have any impact on the bigger picture. And, if that's the only improvement that is made, not much will indeed change on the field. The point, however, is to make many of these small changes until the whole picture of the player looks dramatically different.

There is nothing wrong with having large goals, but those should operate mainly in the background. It's best to be driven forward by small goals that are easy to measure and track. As that work gets done, those bigger goals will start to come into view, and there is no telling what could be accomplished in this game as a result.

EVERY FOOTBALL JOURNEY STARTS SMALL

No one starts out in the Pro Football Hall of Fame. It doesn't matter which legendary player is considered; they all started the same — as a young player trying to find their way on the field. From Tom Brady and Peyton Manning to Patrick Mahomes, Barry Sanders, Emmitt Smith, Troy Aikman, Jerry Rice, and countless others, they all had to follow a path of hard work and consistent growth.

Young players shouldn't get discouraged by how small they feel at first. Football is a big game, and it's easy to feel lost in the shuffle when first getting started. Whether a player has visions of making the pros, playing on a college team, or simply making the high school team someday, everyone has to start somewhere. Most likely, there won't be anything glamorous about that starting point, and the only way to climb the ladder will be to work hard and relentlessly seek improvement and growth.

This book offers an excellent overview of the path that young football players can take, from complete beginner to accomplished player. Of course, just reading a book doesn't really mean anything will be achieved. It's just a foundation. The real hard work begins when the book is put down and the player gets out on the field to do drills, into the gym to lift weights, or in front of the computer to watch film. Sitting on the knowledge offered in this book would be a shame. The magic happens when knowledge is put into action, after all.

It's no surprise that football has a grip on America and won't let go. It's a beautiful game for so many different reasons. Away from the spectacle of the NFL and major college football, there are millions of young players quietly working hard on their skills and gradually improving. Some of those players will go on to reach incredible heights in the game. But for the majority who never step on the field in a huge stadium, the game will still deliver many rewards that will be carried for a lifetime.

www.ingramcontent.com/pod-product-compliance
Lightning Source LLC
Chambersburg PA
CBHW070107080526
44586CB00013B/1223